With Tears and Laughter

An African experience

Leonard V

Photographs by th

All rights reserved. No part of this publication may be reproduced, stored in a retrieval system, or transmitted, in any form or by any means, electronic, mechanical, photocopying, recording or otherwise, without the prior written consent of the publisher and copyright holder.

© Leonard Vear 2009

ISBN 978-0-9563931-0-4

Privately published by the author.

3 Laxton Drive
Kingswood
Wotton-under-Edge
Gloucestershire
GL12 8SQ

Printed in Great Britain by Manor Printing Services, The Manor Group (Wotton) Limited, The Abbey Business Park, Charfield Road, Kingswood, Wotton-under-Edge, Gloucestershire, GL12 8RL

Layout by
Outsource Business Solutions,
52 Parklands, Wotton-under-Edge, Gloucestershire, GL12 7LT

Dedication

For my mother, father and Joan, sister and friend.

Also in memory of Chief Lolik Lado and Manoa, Lui Driver, both of whom were killed in the 1950's troubles in the South. Of the many others I worked with, or met, I have no idea of their fate, but one can hazard a guess.

Also

South of the Avon
Bedminster between the wars
Bedminster Boy
Tales of North Nibley

His 'South of the Avon' was published in 1978 and his autobiography 'Bedminster Boy' in 1980. His well illustrated 'Bedminster between the wars' marks the 50th anniversary of the Bristol and West opening a branch in Bedminster in Cannon Street. Mr Vear did not think of the project he was asked to write, no doubt because of the reputation he has established with his previous sole efforts.
Western Daily Press – November 1981

'Bedminster between the wars' is an era remembered by many still alive today, and one lovingly created by Leonard Vear.
Evening Post – December 1981

List of illustrations

Section One　　　　　　　　　　　　　　　　　　　　　　**Page No.**

1. Group Zanzibar Town 56
2. Tea – Zanzibari fashion 61
3. Group Zanzibar 61
   Ross Innes (rear left) self (rear right)
4. Embarking for Tumbatu 70
   Ross Innes (left foreground) Dr Young (right)
5. Ross Innes with sun-shade 70
6. Group Pemba 77
   (rear row from left) Polish Doctor, Self, Dr Jones, Ross Innes
7. Group Pemba 81
   (front row from left) Polish Doctor, D.C., Self, Ross Innes
8. Andrea – My assistant/interpreter 122
9. Polyneuritic patient – deformed hands 112
10. Patient having old type of injection with 112
    hydnocarpus oil
11. Church – Lui Leprosarium 110
12. Elase 111
13. Schoolboys harvesting Ground Nuts 111
14. Scene near Lui 116
15. Nile at Juba 126
16. Juba Ferry 127
17. Adult grave 163
18. Chief's grave 163
19. Hunter's grave 163
20. Child's grave 163
21. Leprosy village – Luri Rokwe 150
22. Elase and colony scouts 192
    Guard of Honour at wedding

Section Two
Page No.

23.	Andrea examining women and children in Mongalla	179
24.	Gourd carriers	179
25.	Women and girls Mongalla	179
26.	Women and girls	179
27.	Old women	178
28.	Old men	179
29.	Assembling roof of grain store	180
30.	Bodies of grain store	180
31.	Complete grain store	180
32.	'Sausage' tree	179
33.	Man on right carries 'Sausage'	179
34.	Playing 'Holes in Ground' game	179
35.	Long pipe	189
36.	Scene near Lui	116
37.	Patients out-station	203
38.	Old patient out-station	202
39.	Grain delivery out-station	203
40.	Woman kneeling in front of Elase - Lepromatous case	203
41.	Goats on ant-hill	119
42.	Mushroom ant-hill	119
43.	Dokolo's	203
44.	The Hunters	181
45.	Bee-hive	235
46.	Boys on guard	235

Section Three   *Page No.*

47	Boys washing in Nile	232
48.	Nile Steamer & Barges – Terakeka	238
49.	Boy milking – Terakeka	232
50.	Man milking – Terakeka	232
51.	Cattle camp – Terakeka	232
52.	Mandari Hut	235
53.	Dawedi – with Guinea Fowl – Terakeka	242
54.	Farewell Dance	234
55.	Farewell Dance	234
56.	Rest house – Terakeka	239
57.	Mandari Dry Season Camp – Boys wading out into river	239

Section Four – Epilogue   *Page No.*

58.	Scene over looking Lui	250
59.	Gardener with snake - Lui	194

iv

Route from Zanzibar to Juba

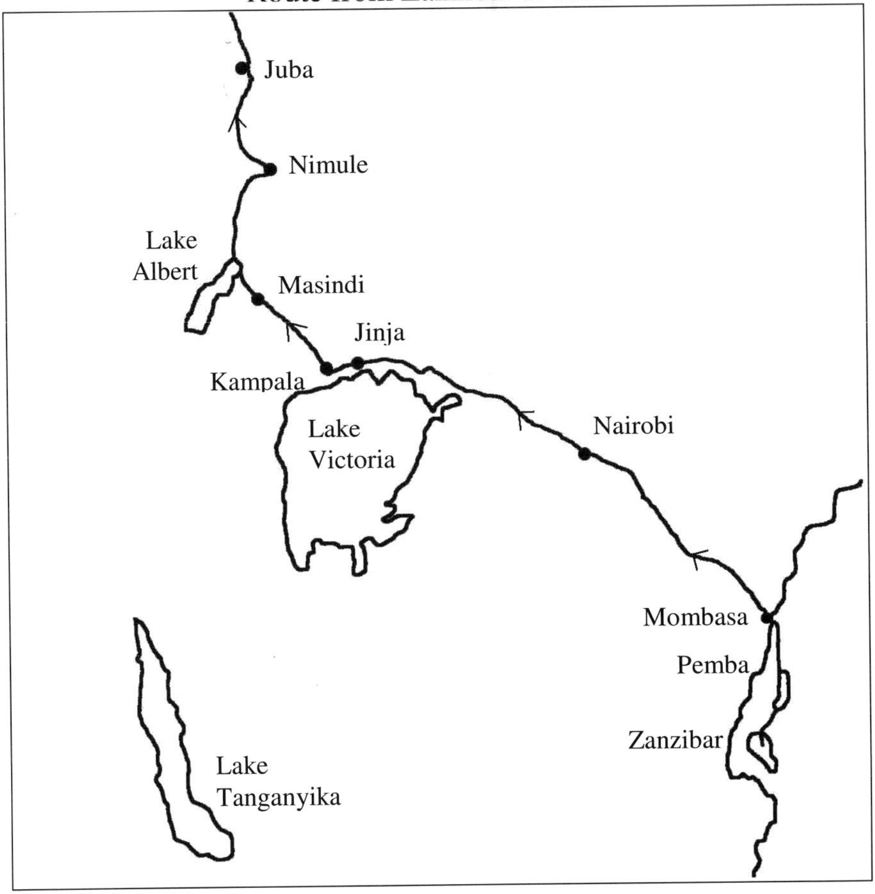

Equatorial Province – S.Sudan

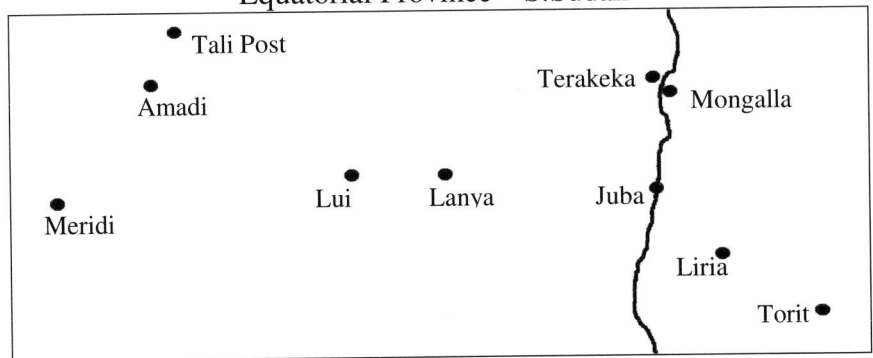

Area of survey

Chapter 1

It could never be the same again.

An inkling of this was forthcoming when, after demob in May 1948, I returned to the Patchway factory of the Bristol Aeroplane Company where I had been serving my apprenticeship, prior to National Service. For two years the Army had attended to my needs as, indeed, I had to theirs. The military life-style had somewhat alienated me from political and economic problems of the outside, civilian world. Leave but a temporary foray into a foreign environment and return to barracks, with its comradeship, at times not altogether unwelcome.

It was this contrast between the two life-styles, the one with its exposure to God's clean air, which struck me as I stepped into the workshop once more. The surroundings were frightening; frankly, I was horrified. Wondering how I had ever become acclimatised to them in those earlier years and feeling very much an industrial Jonah, volunteering for the belly of a factory whale. The natural expectancy of return to 'freedom' was nullified by confrontation with what appeared to be a hell of noise and smell. My lungs encountered an atmosphere contaminated with metal and stonedust, intermingled with steam from coolants and the heavy, blue smoke coiling upwards from overheated cutting oils. Hot, stifling air, blasting out from ducts near floor-level, helped circulate the pollution. My ears were now unaccustomed to the sounds of this industrial disco, with its constant background cadence of rotating shafts and the slap-slap of numerous, endless belts, racing from overhead pulleys to pull into life the floor-based machines. Together with their intermittent hum and rumble and the sporadic shriek of tool-worked metal, the effect was demoralising. Others, who had returned before me, recognised the symptoms - knew the feelings I was experiencing. "Welcome back to the madhouse." they said, with a knowing grin.

And, in addition to this, the world's politicians were at it again. Listening to their reasons for delaying disarmament, whether rightly, or wrongly, made you wonder what had become of the brave new world they had so avidly described but a few years before. Portents suggested we were on the same old roundabout of international bickering, with the cold war hotting up, exposing flimsy relationships born of mutual convenience. The Four Horsemen were still around. Yet, the majority appeared content to pick up the threads of their old pre-war life, satisfied to start afresh with new jobs, new families; thankful to have survived the war. A parochial outlook was taking over once more.

I renewed my friendship with Brian Broad - our childhood escapades have been recorded elsewhere*. During our discussions we both confessed to being unsettled and unable to accept that our lives should continue on the same lines as before. It was Brian who introduced me to Indian philosophy and yoga. Upon gaining a modicum knowledge of Kharma I thought that I had, at last, found an explanation for an incident that had occurred in the Army, the memory of which remains fresh to this day.

Sam Govey and I had gone to bathe in the tidal river near the camp at Fingringhoe, south of Colchester. Unknown to me he couldn't swim. We waded out into the ebbing waters, keeping close to a weathered, wooden jetty. Behind us, on the shore, lay

---

* 'Bedminster Boy'

the tilted bulk of an old, grey-black barge, in the interior of which we had once intruded upon the courtship of one of our officers and his girl-friend. We had made a tactical withdrawal, first on tip-toe and ending in a laughter bellowing stampede.

Suddenly, the gently sloping, sandy-mud underfoot ended and I sank down beneath the water, to surface and gently stroke myself outwards. From behind I heard a spluttering shout of "Help!" Turning, I saw Sam going under with a look of panic on his face. Without much effort I was able to get him back to the shallows, where he spat out a mixture of water and thanks. But next week he was dead - drowned when an assault-boat capsized in a quarry, not far from the spot where I had helped him to safety. But for the toss of a coin I could have been in his place. A point over which I was to ponder, on and off, for years to follow. Some might decry as pointless my questioning "Why?" - saying it is unanswerable. But not to question, not to search for a basic truth, is to sentence one's spirit to atrophy.

Some of the Indian philosophy Brian and I understood well enough, because of similarities to certain tenets of Christianity, but much, at first, was beyond our ken. We turned to the more physical yoga in an attempt 'to open up the various centres of awareness.'

Many of the exercises were undoubtedly beneficial, as were the principles of eating and diet. Several practices appeared rather bizarre and we never attempted them. Such as, by muscular manipulation of the anus, taking up water into the bowel in the form of a self- administered enema. The thought of which has put me off bathing in the Ganges for life. The method was similar to that used by the Frenchman 'Le Petomane' only he took in air, instead of water, as the basis of his art of the musical fart.

While my health improved, relationships with my parents deteriorated somewhat when they discovered that my nightly exercises were causing a patch to wear on the upstairs carpet. I offered to move about the room to even out the wear, but they refused to compromise. So I had to be satisfied with breathing exercises instead - and the odd clandestine position when they were not around.

Two of my uncles, my father's brothers, were working at Displaced Persons' camps in Europe. Having considered this type of work and sensing no real affinity with it, I was left with a vague feeling for some form of social endeavour. During this period of personal, moral vacillation, I chanced upon an article describing the work of the British Empire Leprosy Relief Association - BELRA.

Mention was made of a shortage of lay-workers. Impulsively, I wrote to the Association, enquiring whether I might be considered to work for them. My enquiry was acknowledged and then, to my chagrin, months passed and I heard nothing more. I had, more-or-less, assumed rejection as a prospective lay-worker when a letter arrived - asking if I was still interested and, if so, would I confirm. Light of heart I confirmed by return of post.

BELRA's letter arrived at an opportune moment. During this waiting period of many months I endured moments of despair having, in my heart, already left my toolroom job. Brian voiced romantic plans for going to Paris to live and paint. Unsettled, I inclined towards the idea and together we made tentative plans, going as far as listing our basic needs from items available at ex-service clothing and equipment stores. I casually mentioned these preparations to my mother one evening. I am sure, if physically capable, she would have run up and down the walls of the room. When she calmed down and dried her tears, I came out with the alternative - leprosy work with BELRA overseas. Eventually, because she considered the latter to be 'a real job', in stark contrast to, so she imagined, my diving into a cess-pit of Parisian life, with its aura of orgy, venery and thigh-flashing can-can girls, she became acquiescent to the idea.

Her initial reaction had left me with mixed feelings of frustration and near desperation at the thought of being thwarted by emotional blackmail. I agonised between my own needs and desires and those of my mother. No doubt, had I been an only child, I would have succumbed to her wishes and carried on with my life as before but, as I had a younger sister, the choice was simplified. And too, there followed a sense of relief that the seeds of departure I had sown had received maternal approval - albeit reluctantly.

My return to factory life had been plagued by recurring bouts of septic tonsillitis and eventually it was recommended I have an operation. Upon agreeing to this, and mentioning to my doctor that I was hoping to go overseas in the near future to do leprosy work, he pulled a few strings and I was in hospital within three weeks. Less than two weeks after leaving hospital, while enduring a rather painful recuperation, I received a letter from BELRA asking me to go to an interview in London. Far from fit, my first thoughts were to seek a cancellation of the interview and ask for a later appointment. Then, on second thoughts, considering an opportunity might be lost, I confirmed acceptance.

Arriving at the interview, with what felt like a small hedgehog in my throat, I was confronted by an interviewing panel of three, consisting of BELRA's bearded secretary, Mr Hoare, and two of the Association's doctors. Constantly aware of the discomfort of my throat, I had little time to be nervous. But afterwards, considering I may at times have appeared inarticulate to the panel, I wrote to the secretary, explaining the circumstances. He replied, expressing surprise at the information but confirming, to my relief, that I was still under consideration.

Eventually, early in 1951, I was asked to go to London for a medical and, having passed, was told that later in the year I would be going to Zanzibar to help with a leprosy survey, prior to a survey on my own in the Southern Sudan. From then on at work I savoured the fact that, within a short time, I would be exchanging my present regulated existence for one of challenge and uncertainty.

And, mulling over in my mind what the future might bring, brought back memories of one cold, raw-damp autumn morning, when I was about ten years old. It was dust-bin day and the galvanised containers, together with bags and boxes, stood in line at the gutter's edge, down the length of the street. Most bins contained a high percentage of coal ashes; smoke, drifting upwards from the terraced ranks of houses, confirmed that next week's contribution was being made. I walked the length of the street in a desultory manner, idling away the time until the rest of the gang made their appearance. At the side of Mrs White's dustbin, on the other side of the street, I espied a pile of books tied up with string, set out for disposal. An inveterate reader, albeit mostly of comics and the like, my pulse quickened at what promised to be the chance of a 'find'. With childish cunning I walked on past the books to the end of the street, where I crossed over and made my way back towards them, at the same time keeping an eye open for Mrs White and any other adult for that matter.

Reaching the books, a cursory glance suggested the majority were Sunday School awards. These were of little interest, but a small red-covered book, age-stained yellow at the edges of the leaves, caught my eye. In retrospect there seems little reason why this specific book should have attracted me for the title 'King Solomon's Mines' had, at that time, a biblical rather than a secular connection. I fumbled with the tightly tied string until at last, in desperation, I squeezed my fingers between string and books at one end of the pile and tugged and pulled until white grooves indented my hand. The string gave unexpectedly and the books scattered over the pavement. I had the book of my choice within my grasp when there came a furious tapping at the front-room window of Mrs White's house. I looked up to see her enraged features contorting with unheard admonitions, while her gesticulating hands boded ill.

I raced home, oblivious at first to the book in my hand. My first thoughts were to hide it, so I went up to my bedroom and pushed the book beneath the mattress. No sooner had this been done when there was a loud knocking at the front-door.

"Leonard! See who's at the door." shouted my father from downstairs, having heard me come in a few moments before.

I crept downstairs as the knocking continued. Reluctantly I approached the inner glazed door, with its pseudo stained-glass, through which the shadowy, intimidating figure of Mrs White could be seen. I opened the door slightly, to be greeted by an accusing finger, followed by a tirade of angry vituperation. Attracted by the noise, my father came upstairs to discover what all the fuss was about. Mrs White told her story - hinting strongly that I had taken one of the books. When my father made the point - that did it matter if I had taken one as it was obviously unwanted, I thought myself justified in denying the 'theft', while admitting to scattering the books. Eventually, a justifiably suspicious Mrs White, agreed to be satisfied if I re-tied the bundle.

I read 'King Solomon's Mines' many times in later years, delighting in the adventures of Alan Quartermain, Sir Henry Curtis and Captain John Good. When my trip to Africa was confirmed I indulged in fanciful thoughts of the future, based on the above, together with the atonement of Harry Feversham in the Sudanese adventure, 'The Four Feathers'. Thus, my knowledge of Africa was not only sadly limited, but also grossly distorted. In the interim I did little to remedy this, maybe subconsciously considering that travel alone broadened the mind; sitting and reading about it merely broadened the backside. Instead, I consulted books on leprosy, re-read my old army notebooks on tropical diseases and hygiene and made myself familiar with the world-wide work of BELRA. All this was informative, but lacked practicality. Reading, at times, is like watching a silent film; the personal contact with people, sounds and smells - which may prove very emotive - are absent, and it is these factors which so often affect judgement.

When BELRA gave me a firm date on which to join them I waited a month before my prospective leaving time before handing in my notice at work. When the reason for my leaving was known, it was generally received with disbelief. Some few close acquaintances were surprised, not so much at my choice of work, but the fact that I had not told them before. Others, who had only seen the boisterous side of my nature during my apprenticeship, together with a later outwardly facetious attitude to life, were perplexed. One went as far as to say "I suppose you know you'll be liable to call-up, if you leave?" Thus showing me a hitherto unknown side of his character. However, realising I was still on 'Reserve', I had written to Army Records requesting that should I be re-called I wished to serve in the Medical Corps. Their reply tersely confirmed that should I be required, it would be with the Royal Army Service Corps. The letter was addressed to 'Private Vear.' I had been demoted!

When people questioned my reasons for leaving, I replied I felt the need to do what I considered to be a worthwhile job. But I knew it was due, in some part, to an inner restlessness and a chance to leave an industrial environment. The break for army service had revived memories of the green fields of childhood. And the times when, in my teens, I had walked the paths of Leigh Woods and on to Abbot's Pool, to gaze at its still waters, darkened by the shadowy reflections of bankside trees. Savouring the peace of the moment, away from the city's sounds; feeling the breeze upon my face as it brought into dancing life the limbs and leaves of trees. Bringing too, across the sun-flecked, rippled face of the pool, the sweet scent of Spring flowers. But I was reticent of showing these feelings to others, fearing their lack of understanding and possible ridicule. It is so often much easier to walk these lonely paths with a stranger, than one of longer acquaintance. So I kept this very private world to myself and, in outwardly presenting leprosy relief as the sole reason for leaving my job, eventually convinced myself that this was so.

Farewells were made at work. Farewells to family came later as I would not be sailing until late June. In the meantime, it was up to London - the 'Smoke'. While working as a general dogsbody at BELRA's headquarters I arranged my passage, was indoctrinated, inoculated and vaccinated; the two latter by Dr Cochrane. The cumulative effects of the injections resulted in a feverish night, during which I rolled restlessly from one sore arm to the other, groaning like a banshee. I knew nothing of this myself but was told of it the following morning, by my two room-mates at the Fitzroy Square Toc H hostel where I was staying. Unsuccessfully trying to sleep, they had cursed and wondered what on earth had descended among them, albeit for a short stay, and while my subsequent explanation allayed their fears for the future, they both departed for work strained of expression and heavy-eyed. As one was on shift-work at one of the airports and the other involved with a boy's club in his spare time, I never got to know them very well.

At times the last mentioned helped another boarder, a blind masseur, and several times when he was unable to do so, he asked me to help in his place. It was on such an occasion, one evening, that I helped the blind man to a large block of luxury flats, where the carpeting in the corridors was so thick that you felt you were walking through the carpet instead of upon it. We went upstairs in the lift and made our way to the client's apartment. In answer to our knock a slenderly built, dark complexioned Jew appeared. The masseur explained my reason for being there. We were both invited inside into the long entrance hall, in which stood a solitary table bearing a telephone. A bedroom led off to the right and the blind masseur was taken in there with his equipment, while I was asked to wait in a large room at the end of the hall. In the centre of the room was a piano, its surface gleamingly reflecting a vase of red carnations and several framed photographs. The general decor was expensively tasteful and I sat and quietly enjoyed the atmosphere of the room, predominated by the scent and colour of many flowers. My companion had told me his client was well-known for training singers in voice production, but I was still surprised to see photos of stage and radio personalities displayed on furniture and upon the walls. To most were appended rather flamboyant signatures and extravagant praises.

My thoughts were interrupted by the phone ringing in the hall. I glanced that way as the bedroom door opened. To my slight embarrassment the flat's occupant strode across to the phone, picked it up and stood facing me as he spoke to the caller. He had obviously forgotten I was there and my initial reaction turned to one of amusement - for the man was stark naked, apart from his socks. At last he caught my eye and quickly turned his back on me before I could verify his faith. Then, perhaps considering he was not showing me his best side after all, with bottom twitching and still talking he edged towards the bedroom, to eventually disappear inside.

The more I thought about the incident the more ludicrous it appeared and the silent laughter began. 'Please God', I thought, 'for the blind masseur's sake, don't make me laugh when they come out of the bedroom'. When they did I managed to look non-committal but when we were in the lift, going down, I told my story to my companion, who was not blind to the humour of the situation. We rolled out into the downstairs lobby with tears in our eyes.

I was advised - not altogether wisely - to purchase my equipment in London. In comparison with similar items available abroad most of my purchases were expensive and, in addition, as I was on trek most of the time some were quite unnecessary for my basic needs. In particular was the pith helmet which must have been formed from the same mould as that of the early Victorian explorers. Its appearance on my head drew forth a few humorous remarks, including the rather disparaging 'Missionary Helmet'. It was perhaps understandable, therefore, that being a 'new boy' trying to quietly find my feet in a foreign environment, in more ways than one, I gave it away to one of my boys. In its place I purchased a panama hat which was much lighter and cooler. The bill for my purchases came to £120 - four times my monthly salary. I was deducted between £2 and £3 a month in repayment.

Travel arrangements completed, I was told to help out with the BELRA exhibition, which toured the U.K. It came under the jurisdiction of Bill Berry, an extrovert north-countryman, whose fund raising skills went a long way in keeping the Association solvent. My first assignment was at Cardiff where I was to contact and work with Wally Leach.

It was raining that Friday morning as I left the train at Cardiff Station. Outside I gazed upon the grey dampness of the city, with the distant buildings wet-fogged by the fine rain. To the left of the station entrance lay an area of cleared ground, in the centre of which stood a wind-stirred marquee. I picked my way carefully towards it, alternately overstepping and circling the pools of water scattered over the uneven surface of the ground. A banner secured to the marquee advertised BELRA's exhibition was to be held inside.

I pushed aside the canvas flap and entered, scrunching my way over a heavily cindered floor. In some disarray around the interior walls were exhibition stands displaying information of BELRA's work, together with a history of leprosy; the latter supplemented with photographs of patients and their treatments. Many of the photographs tended towards the more horrific loss of extremities, such as feet and hands, or lepromatus type lesions where the visual impact is much greater than the less obvious tubercular type. But when attention needs to be brought to a problem then the worst side of it must always be shown to establish a sympathetic relationship. Native artefacts brought from all over the world added interest to the general display which was dominated at one end by a large figure, carved from wood by a leprosy patient in West Africa.

Having finished my preliminary inspection of the interior, seemingly devoid of life, I shouted to make my presence known. From behind a canvas screen, at the far end of the marquee, emerged a short, stocky figure. Dark, wavy hair topped a sun-reddened face which, breaking into a welcoming grin, sent wrinkles crow-footing outwards from the corners of bright, blue eyes.

"Wally Leach," he introduced himself, extending a hand. His eyes took in the bag I carried. "You must be Len Vear."

When I had confirmed this, he continued. "Bring your things around the back and I'll make a cup of tea."

Behind the screen was a conglomeration of odd-sized boxes, one of which had been put to use as a table. There were two camp-beds - one in use. Wally indicated the other and I put my belongings upon it. Over tea Wally chatted about the forthcoming exhibition, planned for the morrow, expressing some reservations as to whether it would be ready in time, due to the condition of the site after the heavy rain of the previous day.

"The tent area was awash." he explained. "It was only after I'd trenched to divert the surface water - together with a load of cinders from the council, to build up the floor inside the marquee - that it became feasible to carry on. Let's hope it doesn't rain tonight."

I commiserated with him, then gave a hand with the final placement and lighting of the exhibits. Eventually, late in the evening, we called it a day. As we ate our supper we listened apprehensively to the rain as it was gust-driven against the flapping canvas walls.

I awoke to find Wally shaking me. "You'll have to shift your bed." he said, urgently. "The place is flooding again." And, as I made to get out of bed, he restrained me with "Watch your feet." I looked down. Water appeared to be everywhere and a foot or so from my bed a stream steadily pursued its course towards the far wall. It was a wonder my shoes had not floated away. Half-dressed, our first task was to run a trench across the sleeping area to disperse the more obvious flooding. Inspection of the rest of the marquee showed water coming in from all directions. There was little we could do but wait until first light and hope that the rain had slackened off by then. We brewed up tea and awaited a damp, dismal dawn. Wally's original channels were overflowing so I spent an hour or so deepening them and extending the system some thirty yards or so to lower ground. Gradually the conditions within and adjacent to the marquee improved so that Wally was able to finalize his preparations for the opening of the exhibition later that morning.

During our few days together at Cardiff, Wally Leach told me his reason for joining BELRA. It was totally different to mine, although one might say that there was a similarity inasmuch as we had both been confronted with the question of Why? In Wally's case it had been a blow to the head, whilst serving in the Navy, and from which he had not been expected to survive. With this knowledge, upon recovery, he decided the purpose of his surviving to do God's work. Possibly because of its biblical connections, he chose leprosy relief. But the individual cross he had to bear was that the very thing which had nurtured his belief - a blow to the head - prevented him from working overseas as conditions may have put his health at risk. But he always had hope of going into the field one day, although many gave him little chance. I was delighted, therefore, to meet him many years later at a small outdoor exhibition in Bristol, and to hear that he had gone on a short tour overseas. A triumph for hope and perseverance.

I spent another two days with Wally at the Trowbridge exhibition before going home to say goodbye to my family and friends. Back in London, Bill Berry had me late for the boat-train as we encountered red light after red light on the way to the station. I had barely time to shake his hand as the train pulled away southwards to Tilbury.

I sat in a semi-trance as the train passed the seemingly endless conurbation of London's suburbs, with their distant haze-dimmed, near-featureless buildings; vaguely aware of the near-track small gardens, where line-hung washing waved at the passing train. My feelings were mixed but, generally, the mood was of satisfied expectancy as the metallic drumming of wheel on rail brought me closer to the drums of Africa, as I set off on my time out for life.

Chapter 2

The two-berth cabin on the 'S.S. Durban Castle' was adequate for sleeping and changing, but otherwise cramped for two persons. So, throughout the voyage I rose early, washed and changed and went out on deck before breakfast - weather permitting.

It was here I first saw him, early one morning, standing at the ship's rail, looking as lonely as a Christian prayer in a mosque. Gazing across a green, spume-spattered, heaving sea, which stretched eastwards towards the coast of Spain. Soft-haloed by the early sun, his figure was isolated. I wondered if this air of loneliness was similar to that which I myself was feeling for, as yet, I had struck up no shipboard relationships. Experiencing, as so often in the past, the paradox of wishing to do so, but prevented by a degree of natural reticence with strangers. Not a little envious of those who overcame such situations with social élan and ease.

Going to the rail, a short distance from him, I gazed at the sunlit coastline with lack-lustre interest. My mood dictated I see the land as characterless, devoid of life. After a while, when I caught his eye, we began the usual tentative, desultory conversation of strangers seeking a common interest. He said he was going on the trip around the Cape, then back to England. His sister was living in the south of France and he hoped to see her when the ship put in at Marseilles. Like most people, he was surprised to learn of the purpose of my visit to Zanzibar, volunteering the information that the island was well-known, among other things, for the variety of sea-shells to be found there. Then it was time for breakfast and we parted.

At Gibraltar I continued my casual relationship with my new

companion. Secretly I had christened him 'R.M'. - regarding him as a type of remittance man; restricted in this instance to ship travel, instead of banishment to some far-flung dominion. Walking from the docks to the main street, we were confronted by two unexpected aspects of Gibraltar. The first, a Walls' ice-cream man, complete with stiff cap and striped coat, seated upon his box-fronted tricycle. A sight I had last seen prior to 1939, when a boy. I bought a 'Two-penny-one' and, for once, found the flavour of reality to equal that of memory. As I savoured its coolness a policeman in the uniform of a 'British Bobby' strolled past. My second surprise.

In direct contrast to this familiar sight was the bulky shape of a black-garbed, female fish-seller. She stood in an area of shade near the bottom of a flight of well-worn stone steps, on which was displayed her merchandise. It was a hot day. The sort of day when flies hitch-hiked on anything that moved. That is, unless they had the succulence of fresh fish upon which to retch and gorge. The fish-seller's arms rose and fell to emphasise her spiel; fleshy hands beckoned potential customers to inspect her wares. The action disturbed a multitude of flies and they rose from the fish with a protesting drone. Her physical presence was rather intimidating and I was certain that had I been held by the gaze of those dark, flashing eyes, she would have compelled me to buy her glassy-eyed fish.

I grabbed 'R.M.'s arm and pressed him away before he became well and truly hooked. I had already noticed, in our short walk from the docks, that his air of gullibility had made him an immediate target for touts. Local opportunists saw him as an easy target for their goods; a bird of passage ripe for financial plucking. And, while Helen of Troy's face may have launched a thousand ships, his seemed destined to launch a thousand con-men. I was not altogether sorry when our brief on-shore interlude was over.

At Marseilles 'R.M.' tried to contact his sister. After several unsuccessful attempts I suggested we spend the short time remaining to us exploring the waterfront. To this he eventually acquiesced, obviously disappointed, but persuading himself that his letter to her must have been delayed. I wondered if, perhaps, his letter was the cause of her not being at home!

London's Tower, Wigan's Pier and Marseilles' Chateau d'If have been given some literary significance in fact, fiction or both. The latter now stood before us out in the bay, surrounded by water and now retaining none of the awesome aspect it must once have presented. Under the warm sunshine of a summer's day and a clear blue sky, a myriad array of small boats white-foamed the waters of the bay. The scene evoked a feeling of general happiness and a certain excitement consciously generated by boatmen competing for trade. Near where we stood a sign advertised a trip out to the Chateau d'If.

I looked at 'R.M.' "How about it?"

"Yes - why not. We've plenty of time."

"Better ask the boatman how long the trip takes." I suggested. I was happy to delegate this task to my companion. While, now and then, I recognised words from my school-boy French memory bank, the language for the most part remained as much an enigma as ever. I had overheard 'R.M'. talking to the French telephone operator earlier, when trying to contact his sister, so he obviously had some linguistic ability. Much more than I had anyhow. In reply to the question put to him the boatman smilingly assured us, as he took our money, that the trip would take about three-quarters of an hour. We were happy with this affirmation for that would leave us about thirty minutes in which to return to the ship. Ample time.

The island was a disappointment to me. Of possible interest to a stone-mason, to those nurtured upon 'The Count of Monte Cristo' there was a feeling of anti-climax. There was little left of the outer walls and when the guide indicated a set of sea-air corroded irons, dangling from the grey stone, suggesting they may have secured Alexandre Dumas's hero, you could almost hear the hollow laughter of both author and Edmond Dantes. Perhaps imagination expects too much of reality.

We boarded the boat for the return journey. Before we started the boatman began a rather animated speech, to which the majority of passengers nodded their agreement. Immediately after which the boat-man came among his captive audience and began to collect more money. We were at first perplexed; surely not an advanced tip? 'R.M.' had not got the gist of the spiel. He asked the boatman what it was all about. In broken English he explained, it was for an extra trip around the bay. We tried to explain we did not have the time - we had a ship to catch. He gave a dismissive shrug of his shoulders and started the boat on its way. We sat there both angry and embarrassed, only too aware that some of the other passengers were amused by the situation. Original anger gave way to concern and then near panic. The minutes ticked by as hours. We were trapped on the Bateau d'If!

At last the boat turned towards the shore. Ten minutes remained before sailing time so, as the boat reached the jetty, we did nothing for international relations by shoving our way to the front and leaping ashore. Racing through the streets, we arrived sweaty, swearing (me) and near breathless at the dockside as the ship was signalling its imminent departure with its siren. I spent the rest of the day, until it was time for dinner, collapsed in a deckchair on deck. Oblivious to the hot sun, I fell asleep, and later the throbbing of my face foretold of trouble to come.

My cabin-mate was affable enough. He told me he was 'in civil engineering' and going to Rhodesia. Up to then we had seen little of each other, apart from brief encounters morning and night. The day before we were due to dock in Genoa for a few days he casually mentioned that if I had not made arrangements to go ashore with anyone, then perhaps we might go together. "We could have an Italian meal - I know a decent restaurant."

"I'll see." I answered him vaguely, not wishing to appear churlish. The problem was that I did not have any money to spare for excursions such as this and had already declined the invitation in my mind. There was also the generation gap; with youthful arrogance and immaturity I thought him too old as a companion. He was at least forty! In retrospect I could probably have learnt a lot from him as he had been to Africa several times.

The day we docked at Genoa I had an early breakfast, as usual, then went on deck. Lack of exercise the past few days had left me somewhat jaded. Due, in no small part, to my having to keep out of the sun because of my sunburn at Marseilles. Beyond the town a small range of hills, part haze-hidden, beckoned invitingly.

Looking around the near deserted decks, the need to get away became compelling. Checking I had money in my pocket, I walked down the gangway onto the dockside and, with an increasing sense of freedom, set off in the direction of the hills.

On the northward road out of town large trucks swished by, some pulling trailers, all dragging billowing clouds of fine dust; the latter both clothes-clinging and mouth-parching. This, and the ever increasing heat of the morning sun, contributed to a growing thirst. I began looking for a cafe among the clutter of buildings fringing the road. The way ahead appeared devoid of habitation and here was probably my last chance of a drink. A small delivery-van stood outside a rather unprepossessing looking building. Its function appeared to be that of a cafe, if the posters stuck up outside were anything to go by but, from its general air of seediness, did not hold out much hope for more than a basic service. The door was open but entry impeded by several dozen cords, on which were strung hundreds of metal bottle-tops, hanging vertically in the doorway. Now and then, as the traffic went by, the slight agitation caused by the side-draught disturbed flies resting on the strings.

Brushing aside the bottle-tops I went inside. There was a single low counter, or bar, at which the driver of the van was talking to a woman who had just served him with a drink. Apart from two small posters on the wall behind the bar, extolling the virtues of some drink or another, the rest of the walls were bare. The obviously flirtatious conversation taking place between the two stopped momentarily on my entry. They glanced towards me and, before I could speak, resumed as before. I raised my hand slightly to catch the woman's eye; a little apprehensive that the gesture might be misinterpreted.

Some years before, in Ostend, a friend and I were explaining to some of the locals that our slowness in drinking was not due to illness from our indulgences the night before, but simply that our money had just about run out. Jokingly, we told them we were considering singing in the streets for money. I indicated two of the fishermen with headgear and asked if we could borrow their hats. There was a moment of silence, a quick whispering among themselves, before they all burst out laughing. The daughter of the cafe owner, coming over to find out the cause of their hilarity, heard what the locals had to say, then mirthfully explained that 'Hat', in Flemish, was the term for 'Backside'. So our suggestion was, to say the least, rather unexpected. After leaving the cafe, a little later, we stood outside and warbled a few bars for a while, until we heard an acknowledging shout from indoors.

But here, in Italy, I had caused no offence, committed no faux pas, for the woman just raised her eyebrows enquiringly.

"Coca-Cola, please."

She shrugged her shoulders, obviously not recognising the name of this internationally sold product from my West Country pronunciation. On inspiration I pointed to the driver's drink. She languidly reached under the counter and produced a bottle. I passed over what I hoped was enough money, received some change and taking my drink went close to the doorway, where I had sensed a slight breeze which had somehow managed to squeeze past the iron curtain. The two stood close once more and resumed their conversation. The smallness of the room made me feel like a

Peeping Tom, so I hurriedly drank up and left.

A short distance away the road entered a long tunnel and I had no alternative but to enter. Having gone but a short distance I was soon made aware of my lack of wisdom in taking this route. Lorries thundered through and I spent most of my time flattened against the side wall, shaking from both traffic vibration and fear. I must have come out of there as white as a witchetty grub emerging from rotten wood.

I hurriedly climbed over a low wall to safety. After the comparative coolness of the tunnel the sudden heat came as a shock. I went slowly, then more slowly, upwards; pausing now and then to take a deep, unrelieving breath and stock of my surroundings. Against the hot blue of the sky lay the panorama of yellow-ochre coloured hills, with their sparse covering of sun-shrivelled grass and, snaking into the distance, a thin grey ribbon of highway. At the summit I was able to look back to the town and the sea beyond. I rested awhile in the narrow shade of a low stone wall. A short distance from me was a small recess, its original purpose probably that of some form of shelter. My curiosity overcame me and I half-crawled into its confines, but hastily withdrew. Whatever its original purpose, its latest was obviously that of a toilet. Outside the warm air was positively wine like and fragrant, as it served to cleanse all unpleasantness from my lungs. It was then I noticed an Egyptian half-piastre coin, made of plastic, on the ground. I picked it up and later, back on the ship, some joker told me it was a token for use on the Egyptian underground. He was so persuasive I was half inclined to believe him - not having been to Cairo nor, for that matter, any further south than the north coast of Europe - until he burst out laughing and gave the game away.

Chapter 3

The climb and resulting perspiration had made me thirsty once more. Below was a small house, part surrounded by trees and vines. I made my way towards it and, walking around the side of the dwelling, was greeted by a cloud of dust, stirred by an old woman with a besom. She was dressed all in black, except for the hem of her skirt, which was bordered with light-brown dust, the result of her activities with the broom. Eyes squint-clenched against the dust and sun, she did not see me at first. Moving to one side of the dust cloud I spoke to her. She started - surprised, then turned towards me a weathered face, fine wrinkled like a piece of crazed pottery.

"Do-you-have-water?" I enunciated carefully her eyes flickered over me with an obvious lack of understanding.

"Parlez-vous français?" I persisted.

God knows why I said this. It was sheer stupidity on my part for, even if she did, I had already, with those few brief words, exhausted about five percent of my French vocabulary. But my suggested expertise at French was not to be tested. Somewhat to my relief she shook her head.

I then used up all my Italian in one go. "Aqua." I mimed the act of drinking.

The old lady opened her eyelids slightly, to acknowledge that, at last, she understood my needs. Her mouth gaped to expose, as I had somehow expected, toothless gums, before pointing down the hill and spitting out what I assumed were instructions as to the whereabouts of water. Then, because I hesitated, she seemed to assume I was something akin to an idiot, for she continued more loudly, more loquaciously, and began waving her arms about.

"Merci, madam" I thanked her hastily, retreating in the direction she had indicated, leaving her muttering in her dust.

I followed a well-trodden path downwards until, about fifty yards further on, the footway terminated at the top of a flight of steps. My surprise at seeing these was further compounded by the sight of a rather handsome looking woman sweeping them. She wore what appeared to be the mandatory headscarf, sandals and a loosely tied black kimono. My eyes were drawn to her large, pendulous breasts, free of all restriction, moving beneath the gown. Each sideways sweep of her arm gave the effect of two puppies playing under a blanket. I was appraising this sight when she glanced up and caught me blatantly looking down her substantial cleavage. She straightened and looked me directly in the eye. I felt my face redden and, with a muttered apology, brushed past her without looking back. In my brief experience of life-class I'd never seen anything like that before. Here was no angular, mouth-pouting cat-walk prima donna, but a true descendent of those models portrayed by the old masters; rounded comfortably and made to last. I felt more thirsty than ever.

The small stream flowing past the bottom of the steps seemed to serve a general purpose, for not far away were women washing clothes. I crossed over without stopping to drink; not thirsty enough to tackle the drainings from someone's drawers.

It was getting late so I hurried along. While glancing at my watch I noticed my forearms were beginning to show small, water blisters, proof of the power of the sun on my yet unacclimatised skin.

I discovered also that what I had thought to be long grass, and through which I had been walking somewhat haphazardly was, in fact, scattered stems of oats. Around me people were leisurely cutting the stems and bunching them. Gathering a crop? But, whatever, it suggested the economic state of the area. Then, past the worn-faced tenements of the outer suburbs, balconies decorated with washing, and into one of the main streets leading to the docks.

I was met on board by a somewhat miffed 'R.M.' He explained his attitude by reminding me I had promised to go ashore with him that morning. I did not recall having promised this but did not feel the issue to be worth arguing about. All I wanted was a wash, change and some food. 'R.M.' was still looking rather sour so I suggested we both go ashore later. This cheered him up and he volunteered the information that a crowd from the ship had gone into town to the large modern pool there.

It sounded fun.

After lunch we walked to a large square and tried, unsuccessfully, to discover a way to the pool. It looked as though we were to be disappointed.

"Excuse," a small moustachioed figure stood at my elbow. I groaned inwardly. Not another tout to plague us.

The man smiled. "Excuse," he repeated, "you want swimming?"

I noticed he was looking at our rolled towels and trunks. "Why yes," we affirmed, "we want the pool."

Our new acquaintance pointed across the square to a tram. "For swimming." he said.

We thanked him, shook hands and hurried off to the tram and

were soon under way. What a helpful man!

The pool was supposed to be a short distance from the town centre but, ten minutes further on, there was no sign of it. We began to wonder if we had misinterpreted what we had heard. A few more minutes travel and our worse fears were confirmed, for we were leaving the main part of the town. The sea appeared on our right and it became obvious we had been directed to the beaches. There was nothing but make the most of it, so we alighted at a beach which did not appear too crowded. We soon came to a place which not only sold drinks, but also looked after your clothes and valuables while you were swimming. There was no point in going further with these welcome facilities available. We spent several enjoyable hours swimming and sun-bathing before changing and having a beer before returning to town. Going down the incline to the docks we were accosted by a rather persistent tout who at first wanted to sell us a Parker pen. It was obviously 'Parker' in nothing but name, so we refused. The tout then offered 'R.M.' a better exchange for his money than what he could get officially. 500 lira over the rate. As I stood by helplessly, 'R.M.' pushed his pounds into the other's hot little hands. It was, of course, too good to be true. Back on board we found that one of the notes given in exchange was obsolete and, though it could be changed, was worth 500 lira less that its face value. Not a swindle, but not the bargain 'R.M.' had thought it to be.

But this was nothing compared to the major disaster which had befallen those who had gone to the pool. Without exception all had been relieved of their valuables when swimming. I began to wonder if 'R.M.'s luck was beginning to change.

The following day, after breakfast, (our last day in port) I waited at the gangway for two Scots I had had a drink with the night before. The first, going out to Tanganyika, was in his late twenties; tall, red-faced, big-toothed and out-going. His companion, smaller in build and ten years or so older, was getting off at Mombasa. We had agreed to go together that morning to see one of Genoa's well renowned features, a cemetery containing some finely sculptured tombs.

Then I heard the voice. Everyone meets a 'Voice' at sometime or another, with its raucous, penetrating quality, killing stone dead conversation for yards around. Looking behind I saw to my utter dismay that her entourage contained the two Scots.

"Are you coming with us?" she boomed. As I nodded confirmation the sun seemed to go out of the day.

"Couldn't get rid of her" whispered the Jocks, as we trooped ashore in loose crocodile formation.

We caught a tram to the cemetery which turned out to be sited on the side of a hill. The sculptures were all they were said to be; if anything, better. I tended to linger behind the others at times, when some particular feature demanded more attention. The 'Voice', however, showed little inclination to dwell on individual works. It was while I was studying the craftsmanship which had gone into the nails and veins of the foot of one statue, that I looked up to find the group had disappeared. I went after them, guided by the 'Voice', which went suddenly underground, where it was joined by its own chorus of cacophonous echoes. By the time I reached the spot where they must have entered the vaults, I could no longer hear them. I listened. Not a sound. Surely reverence for the dead had not stilled what I thought only laryngitis could do? There was no point in going on if I did not know which passage to follow. Or, so I argued to myself, here was an opportunity to free myself from what had plagued me all the morning so far and enjoy a little peace. Fragile excuse concocted, and not to take the chance of a further encounter, I retraced my steps back to the entrance of the cemetery. Here were several vendors selling ice cream and various items of trivia.

I went to an ice cream van and, after taking notice of how much people were paying, offered my money for a cornet. The vendor, after searching through his change, looked up and enquired. "Avez-vous dix lira, s'il vous plait?"

I produced a ten lira coin and received a note in change. "Merci" I said, feeling my linguistic oats once more. After all, my mother had always impressed upon me. "It doesn't cost you anything to say 'Thank you'." I then enjoyed the ice cream while awaiting the tram.

It was quite crowded when it arrived and, remembering the fare from the outward journey, I handed over the correct money without comment. Thus hoping to retain some semblance of anonymity and avoid the impeditive tag of 'Tourist'. There was standing room only and pressured forward I was soon hemmed in on all sides. It was hot and uncomfortable and, when the pushing stopped and the journey began, gentle gusts of garlic-tainted breath wafted over my shoulder. In the enclosed, rather claustrophobic atmosphere of the tram, my stomach began to turn over at this unaccustomed, unwelcome after-effect of another's culinary choice. The recently eaten ice cream positioned itself for regurgitation. To forestall impending disaster I adopted a form of shallow breathing, in order to reduce the garlic intake, concentrating on mentally isolating myself from my predicament.

This appeared to work and the feeling of nausea receded. Then, just as I was congratulating myself upon the success of this ruse, I felt suddenly chilled as fingers fumbled at my back-pocket, where I kept my wallet. As my buttocks are rounded, rather than flat and lean, the small wallet was tucked under a curve in the flesh, making withdrawal from the pocket difficult. But this was not deterring the pick-pocket. I wondered what to do. If I grabbed his hand and confronted the miscreant then he, being a local man, might well not only deny the charge, but might even counter accuse me! There could be involvement with the police. The possibilities seemed endless - with little in my favour. Fortunately, I was able to mitigate these fears by the simple expedient of half turning from the person behind and, at the same time, forced myself to avoid eye-contact with whoever it was. Thankfully the ploy had worked. There was no more fumbling at my rear and a soft, prolonged sigh of resignation brought with it an even stronger smell of garlic.

The tram stopped. Sensing the man had left, I glanced through the window to see who alighted. I soon spotted him - but only because he made himself known to me. He could have merged into the crowd quite easily. Wearing a cap and a slight smile on his tanned, short-bristled face, he stood about six feet from the window and looked directly at me. When certain of my attention, his smile increased and he slowly shook his head from side to side, acknowledging his lack of success. I could not help returning his smile; gently nodding my head to confirm I'd got the message.

As the tram sped on its less malodorous way, I realised the man had been the source of the garlic breath. I mused over the supposition that, as money was his object, I would have quite happily have given him some to have breathed the other way.

The others received my excuse for leaving the cemetery without them with exaggerated expressions of disbelief. I thought they might. Relating my experience on the tram overcame their derision to a great extent, and they had a good laugh at my expense.

That evening, after dark, I went ashore with the younger of the two Scots as his wife had asked him to get her a fan. Of course, before we left a few helpful souls expressed the hope that we were cognisant with the dangers awaiting young men wandering up dark side-streets in foreign ports.

"Ignore the girls," we were advised. "Or their pimps might have you".

Though we laughed at this we were both a little apprehensive, knowing there was some truth in what was said. We felt relatively safe in the better-lit streets, but hurried along quickly when white faces, voicing accented invitations, materialised out of the shadows. Jock finally made a purchase and we wasted no time on the return journey. I estimated there must have been as many fannies for sale as fans.

Next morning we sailed for Port Said.

Chapter 4

The following day saw me leaving the land of the Romans with a face resembling a tessellated pavement. What had once been a smooth, golden mahogany tan had deteriorated overnight into patches of sunburnt skin; interlaced with cracks and showing, by the pinkness of new epidermal growth, that nature was doing its best to put to rights my self-inflicted wounds. It was not a pretty sight. There was really nowhere to hide - unless I became a seafaring hermit in my cabin. Exposing myself to the public in this sorry state, I could see people appraising my condition. Their expressions showing sympathy, amusement or, 'Serve you damn well right.' The tan, which others had commented upon, not without envy, but a few days before, was dying a rather sordid death. My ego trip had ended. I was obliged to sit in the shade, with cream on my face to alleviate the soreness. It had to be one of the Scots, of course, who first came out with the remark "You're cracking up."

'R.M.' was not interested in shipboard games. After the tournaments began I saw less and less of him, eventually becoming attached to a group containing the Scots and two Australian girls and their mother.

Told of the blueness of the Mediterranean I had taken the rather glib description with a pinch of sea-salt. So it was with something akin to wonderment that I gazed upon those waters for the first time and, from that point on, found their blue placidity soothing - if not hypnotic. This effect helped in no small way by having the youngest of the Australian girls next to me at the ship's rail. Now and then nature's deception became apparent at the sight of pale, green water sliding by the side of the ship. Under dark clouds, instead of a sky of serene blue - what colour then? We never found out for the days remained sunny and hot, as we continued in our own small world of ship, sea and sky.

After the deck games had been in progress for a while, I found myself in the quarter-finals of the deck-quoits, deck-tennis and darts. In the first-named my heart sank when I saw my opponent's name - it was the Yugoslav, a hot favourite to win. I'd seen him play and had played him unsuccessfully myself. Without a doubt he was good; his technique unusual. Whereas most players set the quoit skimming along the deck to slide into the scoring circles, he lobbed the quoit high into the air, so that it came down flat without skidding on. 60% of the time he could land it on the centre circle, often covering it completely. This was made possible by the fact that the 'quoits' being used were rubber discs, about eight inches across and three-eighths of an inch thick. It was difficult to get a good 'strike' when skimming these along the deck at speed to remove a scoring quoit. Had we played with the usual rope deck-quoit his technique would not have been successful, due to this quoit's tendency to bounce and slide upon landing. He would have been forced to play a more conventional game.

On the morning of the match I reported on deck to be told by one of the games' organisers that, because of a backlog of matches, we would have to play on a pitch situated beneath the upper deck, instead of in the open. It made no difference to me, but the Yugoslav complained bitterly when told. I kept out of the argument; the situation looked like becoming unnecessarily nasty. My opponent's objection was quite naturally, because of his method of play, against the lowness of the deck. The organiser pointed out that no one else had complained - so why should he? Either play - or forfeit the match. Inwardly, I was celebrating my good luck at this favourable turn of events, so that when I was asked whether I had any exception to playing, I replied quite happily "Not in the least."

The Yugoslav grumbled throughout the match and I am sure that some of his barely audible mumbling, had it been interpreted, would have shortened the match with a disqualification. His expression was as dark as his hair when he saw his usually winning lobs hitting the over-head structure, to fall short; or hit the target and slide on. He was not a happy man. After a short while it became obvious that he had given up. He stomped off at the end without offering the usual congratulatory handshake. Not that I deserved one as the game had been a farce. I played the semifinal later that day and lost.

That evening I was sitting in the lounge with June, one of the Australian girls, sucking up a glass of passion-fruit juice. I must confess I had first tried this drink rather hopefully, but soon resigned myself to its thirst quenching qualities only. The Yugoslav came across to our table and asked if he might sit down. I wasn't enthused with the idea but nodded a reluctant assent. At first he made small talk, mainly directed at my companion and then, when the conversation flagged, he suggested I help him with a trick. Disinterestedly and without thinking, I agreed.

I was to hold two matches against the sides of the box, by the heads, with thumb and forefinger. A third match was then placed between the protruding ends of the matches and held in position by the pressure exerted by the other two against the box.

"Hold it until I count to ten." he said.

I tensed my fingers as he slowly began to count. Just before he reached the count of 'ten' he slammed his hand down hard against the matches, causing them to slide down the abrasive surface and ignite.

I was unable to withdraw my fingers quickly enough; for a moment the pain was near unbearable. The Yugoslav collapsed with laughter at the success of his 'trick', while I felt myself flush with anger for being so naive.

"You like the trick - yes?" He grinned broadly.

"No." Lips stiffened with anger it was all I could say in reply. If I had remained there any longer, looking at his taunting expression, I felt I would explode. So, glancing across at June, I indicated that we leave. He remained there, obviously happy with his revenge for my having beaten him at quoits.

I found myself playing the Greek in the darts semi-final and, after my experience with the Yugoslav, made a mental note to be beware of gifts. Judiciously, the day before the match, I considered my opponent's play from a distance, observing with sinking spirits his air of professionalism. Effortlessly he sent his darts into their target. It appeared my only chance of winning was if he became handicapped overnight with broken or festering fingers. The evening prior to the match I took another look at the order-of-play list. To savour, I suppose, my near moment of glory, which was now receding as it had already done so with the deck quoits and deck-tennis.

Then, I could scarcely believe my eyes - the Greek's name had been crossed through. Apparently he was unable to compete because of leaving the ship at his destination the following morning. When the ship stood off the Greek coast early next day, I went on deck to watch my would-be opponent disappear in a launch around the headland of a rocky bay. Later, I played a young lad with whom I had many a friendly match, in the final, managing to scrape through for a win. At the prize-giving, amid the usual sarcastic applause, I collected my prize. The shipping line obviously believed the honour of winning to be far greater than pecuniary gain. I opened my envelope to find a five shilling token - to be spent on board ship. June and I shared a few glasses of passion-fruit juice and got rid of it.

Now that the competitions were over, there was time to relax and take note of the passengers who seemed as strangers. One, a young Egyptian girl, was something of an enigma. Never alone, but always accompanied by two male escorts with the build of harem eunuchs. The two appeared to be bodyguards of some kind, for they seldom ever spoke with the girl conversationally, nor did they behave towards her as would a friend. She seldom smiled. No one knew who they were for the men's air of restrained hostility did not encourage casual social contact. The three remained a mystery to the end.

Another Egyptian passenger was of a more gregarious nature. He came to my side as I was looking shorewards, the day before we were due to dock at Port Said. Well-built, standing over six feet tall, with dark curly hair and a small moustache. When he smiled he displayed a set of teeth that made you feel embarrassed to smile too broadly in return.

"Are you going ashore tomorrow?" he enquired

"Yes. It will make a break."

"Have you been here before?" he continued.

I admitted it was my first time.

"Then," he said, releasing his smile, "if you would like to come ashore with me, I'll show you around." He looked at me enquiringly for an answer.

I wasn't at all comfortable with his suggestion. It was so unexpected, but I could think of no expedient excuse for refusing outright, without causing possible affront which I did not, of course, intend. There was a certain fascination about the idea so, pushing my doubts to one side, I tentatively agreed to go with him. Adding the proviso, "All being well".

He nodded at my acceptance and seemed pleased, going on to tell me that he was a pilot in the Egyptian Air Force. We spoke of general things for a while before I made an excuse and left him. After we parted I wondered if there was a white slave traffic in males. And the double entendre of wartime 'Target for tonight' for some reason came to mind.

I was making my way to the disembarkation point the following day when I was approached by a young Yorkshireman who was returning, with his wife and small child, to Rhodesia.

"Are you going ashore?" he asked. Rather hopefully I thought. When I nodded he added hurriedly, "Would you mind coming with us?" He indicated his wife and push-chaired child. "The wife's wary about going ashore alone."

Looking down upon the seething mass of anticipatory touts, mendicants and goodness knows what else, I could see her point of view. It was rather intimidating. Glancing back along the deck of the ship I saw no sign of the Egyptian pilot.

"I was supposed to be going..." I began, but left my explanation unfinished when I saw the growing looks of disappointment on their faces.

"All right." I conceded, "I'll come with you." And was overwhelmed by their profuse thanks, out of all proportion to the occasion.

Into the maelstrom of vociferous Port Saidians, or Port Sadists, if the lethal looking leather-bound coshes were any indication of their morality. The character attempting to sell us these matched us stride for stride as we forged a path through the crowd. He also sold hunting-crops and postcards. The latter, he suggested, of a stimulating kind. But with deference to my companion's wife I managed to prevent him taking them out from under his robes. Slender ivory and wooden backscratchers were available for those plagued by lice or fleas; or women with itchy bra.

It was all rather confusing and we found it impossible to stop to inspect goods and stalls, to do so was to invite all manner of fast-talking vendors, waving their wares in your face. Doggedly we kept going, glimpsing now and again small groups of fellow passengers experiencing the same difficulties as ourselves. In a more open part of the thoroughfare we came across a Gully-gully man - one of those impressive Egyptian conjurors. The trick he was performing so expertly, when we joined the group around him, was that of introducing small chicks into the shirt fronts of male bystanders, to the astonishment of all when the unknowing participant withdrew the bird. I checked my wallet. If he could put things into your clothes it stood to reason he could also remove objects with stealth. It was still in my possession but I checked behind me now and again, to be sure, on our way back to the ship.

I saw June now and again as we struggled through the crowds and back on board we exchanged experiences. I showed her the tassel-topped fez I had been persuaded to buy.

"One of the men offered to sell me a pair of automatic pyjamas." She looked at me innocently. "What are they?"

My imagination went into overdrive but I forced myself to subdue my fantasies and, with a shrug of the shoulders, suggested she must have misheard the man. I have wondered since what they really were.

It was after dark when I suddenly remembered my promise to a young lad at home to get him some foreign stamps. Once more I went ashore into a now darkened environment and one in which I did not intend to dally too long. First stop was Simon Artz, a large store not far from the docks. Inside I walked between row after row of glass-topped display cases; to finally purchase a small ivory bracelet as a present.

Approaching the main post-office, I was accosted by what appeared to be an Egyptian version of Fagin, with wheedling voice, hooked nose and straggling beard. He carried a tray around his neck on which were displayed numerous packets of used stamps. In the diminished light away from the post-office I could see, through the cellophane window of the packet, that it appeared to contain a fair selection of stamps. Reasonably priced too. I stood for a moment undecided.

While thus I felt a hand rubbing against my arm and a rather husky voice, twinned with a drink-laden breath, informed me that the owner of these rather undesirable attributes was certain I was going to give her some 'Rhodesian pounds'. Turning, I was shocked to see a white woman at my side. For a moment I was at a loss as to what to do. The stamp dealer solved my problem by shouting at the woman and pushing her unceremoniously away. Obviously used to this type of treatment, she murmured something and retreated back into the deeper shadows. Hurriedly I took several packets of stamps at random from the tray and made my way back to the ship.

At the docks' entrance a small group of the ship's crew were swaying home after drinking in the local atmosphere ashore. One, lagging behind the rest, was delayed by a figure which insidiously detached itself from a wall. A deal was apparently made and the local hurriedly made off. The sailor's companions gathered around him to see what he had bought. He withdrew photograph after photograph out of a packet, to his increasing bewilderment and his friends' rising mirth.

"The bugger!" he slurred, turning to see if the salesman was still there. "He said they were French photographs." It was pointed out to him that they were. Even though each one was of the Eiffel Tower.

I told the others about the incident when I returned and they had a good laugh at the sailor's expense. I did not tell them however, that upon opening my packets of 'foreign stamps' I found most of them to be small value British and what Egyptian there were were greatly duplicated. And the ivory bracelet turned out to be plastic.

The Gully-gully man gave a show on board that evening. I wondered if he used the same chickens as he had previously and whether he hypnotised them in some way to keep them quiet. Unless the close proximity to sweaty arm-pits was enough to silence their natural chirpiness.

The ship had travelled slowly down the canal and, because of the closeness to animals and habitation, the flies invaded us constantly. A pest from which we had been free at sea.

Our voyage continued down the canal until we emerged at the Bitter Lakes. Here, a clutter of ships of all shapes, sizes and nationality awaited their turn to enter the southern or northern section of the canal. After some delay, which was not altogether unpleasant as a slight breeze came across the open water, we entered the lower canal to exit in the Red Sea.

We made landfall at Port Sudan and, like true tourists, took a glass-bottomed boat out over the coral reef and looked down through the clear water with something like awe upon the multi-coloured, multi-formed outcrops of coral. Richly coloured, but further enriched by the tropical fish dawdling, or darting in groups with synchronised movement in a kaleidoscopic mass of colours. We were fascinated by this natural aquarium, for it was an era before television's ubiquitous nature programmes made the uncommon commonplace.

Told of a swimming pool ashore for the exclusive use of seamen, we thought we might be allowed in. The man at the entrance thought not and directed us down the road to the public pool. Having come this far we were reluctant to forgo the chance of a swim. Upon entering the confines of the pool the girls took one look at the water and said they preferred to drink their soup, rather than swim in it. Its potential as a health hazard must have been high. A fact brought home to us when our feet encountered slime on the bottom of the pool, posing the question as to what pestilence was being encouraged to fecundity under the hot sun. The warm water became rather unpleasant and far from refreshing. We remained there just long enough for me to sustain a fractured toe. This was the result of a ginger-haired, lanky Scot lashing out at me in a splashing contest. He may have walked with the gait of a camel but he had a kick like a mule. Unable to secure my sandal properly, I flip-flopped my way back to the ship, enduring the heartless ribbing of the others.

At Mombasa, the few days we were there, I limped my way along the main street, where vendors of fruit and vegetables were hugging the pavement on the left-hand side. At the far end of the thoroughfare, facing a rank of rickshaws in the centre of the road, with their languid owners emerging from a heat induced trance-like state at the chance of a fare, were the wood-carvers, goods displayed before them on the pavement.

Prominent on the shoreline were the eye-dazzling, white-walled remains of the old Portuguese defensive position, Fort Jesus, with its wide view seawards. Not far away was a low walled garden, rather overgrown, and lying among roots and low leafy growth were the shells of the giant African snail, a meal in themselves - if you like that sort of thing.

June and I edged our way along the narrow path leading from the fort and skirting the rocky shoreline, enjoying the heat of the sun, tempered as it was by an onshore breeze. Here, the sea waved at the rocks, prior to making a lunge of foaming intrusion and flinging itself skywards in a cloud of sun-kissed spray. As we gazed at this billowing cloud of mist, its nebulosity was suddenly transformed as the shape and colours of a miniature rainbow were held there; fading as the droplets dispersed. This phenomenon was repeated again and again, when sufficient spray was hanging high, but the initial joyous experience retained its uniqueness. The magic of this moment has always remained for, when circumstances combine with senses they sometimes create an impression surpassing imagination. Even to raise doubts as to what you had hitherto considered to be ultimate reality.

As the waters receded from the rocks, small crabs scurried back to the lower reaches and where, no doubt, they fed upon what had been deposited by the tide. A rather precarious activity and one which appeared to be more consuming of time than food.

At this end of the town there was also an Indian-run cinema. The film showing was 'Robin Hood'- starring Errol Flynn. Still finding walking difficult, with the damaged toe, June and I decided to attend the afternoon performance to sit down for a while. We entered the cinema and were directed to the rear seats over which, we were happy to note, several long-bladed fans were introducing coolness into an otherwise warm atmosphere. The seats in our immediate vicinity were empty but those at the front were packed with a murmurous audience, buzzing with the excited expectancy of a Saturday morning picture show crowd at home. The film was in colour - the audience black and white.

A small feature film began the programme. An old film, but who apart from us was to know. Its star was an American archery expert who, after demonstrating his prowess at straight-forward bowmanship, went into his programme of tricks. I don't know how many retakes they had to make, but his marksmanship was perfect. Not only did he fire arrows singly, but also in pairs. One arrow soared into the bullseye on one target while the other burst a balloon on the second. All good stuff and then, after firing over his shoulder with his back to the target, using a mirror, he bent down and fired two arrow between his legs into targets. As there was no precautionary warning about the dangers of attempting some of these tricks, it was quite possible, in the case of the latter, to perform the forerunner to a vasectomy.

It could not have been a coincidence that this film was shown on the same programme as 'Robin Hood', someone knew their audience psychology; how to bring the impossible within the realm of probability. Flynn's exploits with the long-bow were received with delight, even though many were akin to flights of the imagination than that of arrows. His splitting of his opponent's arrow in the archery contest was acknowledged with noiseful acclaim. We were as much amused by the antics of the audience as we were with those of Flynn.

I had arranged to have five pounds sent from my bank in England to the one in Mombasa. This amount may appear insignificant but, in 1951 it was just short of a week's average wage in the UK. Come our last day in Mombasa this had all but gone. I was faced with the decision of spending most of what remained on a meal ashore, or eking it out until we arrived at Zanzibar where, I had been told by the London office, there awaited me fifty pounds - for hotel expenses etc. The problem was resolved by June finding a ten-shilling note floating about the deck. We took it with us to town and it paid for a meal and the hire of a rickshaw back to the ship.

We had a brief stop at Tanga, which lay in Tanganyika Territory, just over the border from Kenya. As the ship was obliged to anchor out in the bay a party of us went ashore in a launch. After landing we went to a hotel recommended to us and one which appeared to cater for British expatriates. The dining room was atmospherically British, from the pictures on the walls to the cane furniture and a large piano. Only the view from the window proved the foreign environment.

I sat near the piano with a glass of squash in one hand a cigarette in the other. A woman in the party, whom I had not seen before, came up to me and said, over-loudly. "You've got artistic hands - will you play something for us?" My hands had done a lot of things in their time, but playing the piano was not one of them. She asked again, obviously thinking I was shy of displaying my talent. She eventually went away, not entirely convinced, leaving me self-consciously thinking that everyone was looking at my hands. I was glad they were occupied, otherwise I would not have known what to do with them.

The general conversation became rather trite and uninteresting; my thoughts turned to Zanzibar and the future. I felt I had to get away from this confining atmosphere, so asked June if she would like to go for a walk. She agreed and we made our way down the road which meandered through the small town of Tanga, with tall palm trees standing like sentinels on either side, cross-hatching the road with their slender shadows. A dog suddenly rushed out into the road into the path of a native cyclist. He couldn't avoid the animal and the dog, after an initial yelp, crouched whimpering on the dusty road. The cyclist disappeared. I went over to the dog to see if there was any obvious injury. There seemed to be some damage to one of the forelegs. Suddenly there was a scattering of onlookers as a loud-mouthed, teen-aged white girl pushed me to one side and, picking up the dog, she proceeded to generally upbraid those standing nearby. Obviously someone who used buckshot instead of the discriminatory bullet. Before I could point out the dog's injury she strode off in the direction of one of larger houses, alternately comforting the dog and cursing all cyclists. I could see now why the involved cyclist had lost no time in disappearing down the road. He'd probably recognised the dog.

Somehow, for me, the incident cast a shadow over the afternoon, so we left the vicinity and made our way down to the rather desolate beach. Here, we found the corpse of a beaked parrot-fish lying on the white sand, its coral crunching days over. Flies were enjoying a walk-over inspection of their meal before it was removed by the next tide. The end of a life. The end of an era. The end of a voyage for next day we docked at Zanzibar. As we strolled without speaking over the hot sand, my thoughts once more turned to the immediate future. And soon there would be farewells to those I had met on the voyage. For a moment I felt a sense of near sadness, then it passed and normality returned.

"Come on." I urged. "Race you back to the others."

Chapter 5

Morning of arrival my baggage was packed in readiness for leaving ship. With the exception of a large trunk in the hold, which I was assured would be landed later that day and could be collected from the agent. Standing on deck, I contemplated the passing scene; squint-eyed, as the low-hung sun's light reflected back from the mirror-faced, gently tremulous sea. Fronted by long, silvery beaches, the tall palms of the shambas[*] stood sharply etched, in dark-green silhouette, against the clear pastel blue of the morning sky. The island looked the complete tropic paradise. As we drew nearer to the docks the smell of the sea was superseded by the combined scents of copra, cloves and other spices. Sacks of these commodities were stacked in, or near, the dockside warehouses. Thus, you were made aware immediately of Zanzibar's chief exports.

As I had been told I would be met by a member of the Zanzibar Medical Service, I stood at the top of the gangway so as not to miss whoever it was. The launch came and went, taking people off and bringing others aboard. Eventually, after the launch had returned once more, I heard my name mentioned and made myself known to the enquirer. He, in turn, introduced himself as Dr Keith Young. Without further delay we returned ashore and loaded what luggage I had into his car. My companion drove slowly down the road leading from the docks, stopping now and then to avoid work-gangs hauling carts which were high stacked with sacks of produce. And, as the sweat fell from the labourers'

---

[*] Small plantations

straining, glistening torsos, there arose from their throats the ubiquitous work chant of Africa.

Away from this hive of commercial activity we passed the island's more picturesque waterfront and where, facing an uninterrupted seaward aspect, stood the dominating, white-gleaming palace of the Sultan of Zanzibar. Arab authoritarian rule, now tempered somewhat by international disapproval and commercial necessity, had once made the trade of slavery its major enterprise. Where the tourist was now greeted by the aroma of spices, around the turn of the century they would have been assailed by the stench of over-packed dhows bringing potential slaves from the African mainland. For, after the slave trade to the Americas had been broken, traders transferred their lucrative operations to a new base at Zanzibar. The trade flourished at this centre from the early part of the 19th century to a decade into the 20th. Yet much later, without knowledge of this, it was easy to assume that the island had never suffered man's baser instincts. That there had been no snakes in this 'Garden of Eden'.

Dr Young explained, when we arrived at the Zanzibar Hotel, that I would be staying here for a couple of nights only and then it had been arranged I should then sleep at his house, having my main meals only at the hotel. He then left, saying he would contact me the following morning.

As soon as I had put my baggage in my room I left the hotel and returned to the 'Durban Castle'. Here, I picked up June and we went ashore. I went to the bank to withdraw money from the deposit BELRA had said would be awaiting me. The clerk I spoke to could find no record of the transaction and suggested I call back the next day. Frustrated and denied my intention of a brief excursion together, we returned to the hotel for tea before returning to the ship, where I remained until late evening. After I had said my farewells, I found, to my consternation, that I did not have the fare for a rickshaw to take me to my hotel - so I had to borrow money from June. It had not been my day.

Descending the gangway I looked back to where June stood at the exit point. We waved to one another and then, suddenly, she was gone. As we neared the shore, from a distance the dancing reflections of the ship's lights on the water gave the impression of a ship floating upon a sea of sequins. Looking at the comparative darkness of the dockside, now that the activity and warmth of the morning were absent, I felt depressed at the severing of a shipboard relationship which had come to mean so much.

The rickshaw deposited me in the hotel courtyard, beneath a small clump of palms. Stopping briefly at the desk for a tin of cigarettes I went straight upstairs to bed. In my absence the bed had been made up and the mosquito net tucked in all round. On the small bedside table was a jug of water and a glass, which reminded me to take a paludrine tablet before getting into bed. For a while I remained sleepless, disturbed by latecomers arriving and others leaving just below my window. And then, when this activity ceased, the unaccustomed sound of the palm leaves' dry rustle as they were stirred by the evening breeze delayed sleep a little while longer.

The following morning about 9.30 am Dr Young called and together we went to the Medical Centre, where I was introduced to Doctor Tallack, the Medical Officer of Health. As a visit was just about due to the small leprosarium attached to the Roman Catholic Mission at Walezo, it was arranged that I go there with the two doctors. My feelings were mixed at visiting Walezo at such short notice, for I had not seen the effects of leprosy at first hand. The doctors were probably unaware of both my lack of practical experience and my feelings of unease at this earlier than expected confrontation, for which I was totally unprepared.

When we arrived at the Mission the nuns were quietly friendly and, escorted by one of their number, we walked to the red-brick dispensary. Here the young Belgian sister rang a bell. From the shadows of grass roofed huts, fronting the palm-lined dirt road which ran through the centre of the grounds, figures slowly emerged into the sunshine. They made their way towards the assembly point where we awaited them.

My pulse quickened at their approach and then, as they drew nearer, their nodular disfigurements and deformities of feet and hands could be clearly seen. When they crowded around, acknowledging our greetings, my face must have surely betrayed my inner thoughts of repugnance and disgust. I fought against nausea at the unaccustomed stench from their bandages and wound coverings. Feeling enveloped by the physical aspect of the disease, I tried not to breathe the still, humid air of the small dispensary, containing as it did the exhalations of the patients. This was cold fact, with all its implications, not clean, clinical, text-book photography; here and then I experienced the initial shock of atmospheric reality. The first doubt of my choice of leprosy work made so many months before in the convivial environment of England, began. Would I ever accept these afflicted people as people?

The sister was smiling at the arrivals, but in spite of the warmth of her smile the disturbing emotive coldness remained inside. This was not helped by Dr Tallack asking me to feel the enlarged ulnar nerve of one of the patients. This condition often confirming a diagnosis. Afterwards I rather hastily washed my hands in the bowl supplied for that purpose.

It was certainly most unfortunate I should have been confronted, at this stage, with such extreme ravages of leprosy; but leprosaria invariably hold these types of cases. Had I been gradually introduced to the disease, in the course of survey work, where the slight and sometimes barely discernible cases were prevalent, my experience would not have been anywhere so traumatic.

Dr Young specialised in tuberculosis and on one occasion took me with him into the hills where there was a small isolation hospital for his patients. I suppose, at times, the Medical Service were at a loss as to what to do with me until Ross Innes' arrival and the brunt of this fell upon Keith and Marie Young, after I moved into their home. It was a typical Arab-style building, two-storied and squarish in structure, with whitened outer walls. You entered via a massive wooden door, brass studded, but not ornately so, into a long hall from where the family's living and sleeping quarters were reached by a flight of stone stairs. Across the street the island's courthouse fronted a fairly spacious square, itself a junction for the streets and alleys leading into it from all directions.

One evening, Dr Young took me along to the European Club. I had no formal tropical attire, having considered it an unnecessary expense when kitting out in the UK. I made do with a white shirt, khaki-drill slacks and black shoes. As we entered the club one of the members looked frankly aghast at my casual dress and remarked to his drinking companion, in a voice deliberately loud enough for all to hear:

"Who on earth's THAT?"

Other members turned to stare at 'THAT' and I flushed with embarrassment. At that moment there was a distraction as a drunken Irish woman slid along the bar, breaking several glasses in the process. I heard a soft murmur of "Paddy's at it again" but, for the most part, her behaviour was politely ignored. The tolerance of social equals.

Dr Young bought me a drink and diplomatically took me outside on the balcony, where he introduced me to Lady Somebody or Other who was interested in the forthcoming leprosy survey. There was little I could tell her at this stage for I knew nothing of Ross Innes' plans, nor his method of working. This short discussion over, I fell into a state of self-deprecation, occasioned by the initial rudeness I had encountered upon entry to the club. After a series of silences in our conversation, which gradually became longer, she quite rightly became bored with me and making an excuse left me alone at the table. Seeing Dr Young just inside the doorway to the bar, I begged to be excused and returned to his house to the companionship of his small library.

My embarrassment at the club was mitigated to some extent when, after Ross Innes' arrival, we were both invited to dinner with the Youngs and their friends. Ross Innes turned up in a thin linen suit with very fine pink stripes. Even I looked at it twice. Once, when he left the room, his attire was the subject of amused comment, with the speculation that he had come in his pyjamas. But if Ross Innes had noticed the others' glances (and it was impossible for him not to have done) he remained quite unperturbed. He was his own man and I was pleased we conformed in one respect - our nonconformity in clothes. The situation never bothered me again.

Marie Young belonged to the Zanzibar Amateur Dramatic Society, which staged plays on a casual basis. I went along to see a creditable performance of 'The Ghost Train', which was attended by a racially mixed audience. The show was late in starting as the Sultan of Zanzibar was to attend. The Zanzibari National Anthem suddenly sounded out from the wings of the stage - played on a gramophone. As suddenly as it had begun it stopped, and those rising to their feet sat down again. Almost immediately the scratchy rendition of the anthem began again and everyone scrambled back on their feet. This time the Sultan made his entrance and, after a brief introduction to several people, he sat down in the front row. Everyone had stood in silent obeisance during this and the anthem grated on. I wondered if, and rather maliciously hoped, the needle might get stuck in the groove, to turn the show into one of musical comedy.

Other activities of the European expatriates were cricket, tennis and golf or, for the more adventurous, diving along the outer reef. The golfers were in an on-going state of environmental warfare with local cattle owners, whose beasts' natural functions set up convex bunkers on the greens.

At last, Dr Ross Innes arrived and I viewed our first meeting with some trepidation. Not without cause, for he was one of the world's most experienced leprologists, having worked in the Pacific islands, India and latterly in Africa, where he held the post of Interterritorial Leprologist for Kenya, Rhodesia and Uganda. Against this formidable background I felt rather inadequate. But my fears were unfounded when, from the start, this out-going, red-faced and red-headed Scot put me at my ease.

Zanzibar Town was our first work area and the survey began here on the 16th July 1951. The survey was intended to be an intensive one, involving as many of the population as were conveniently available, with samples taken from as many places as was contingent. Under the most equable conditions a uniform proportion of adult males, females and children would have been examined but here, in Zanzibar, an examination of the women was not insisted upon because of the strong Islam influence. Conversely, this problem was not encountered on Pemba Island, where adequate numbers of women volunteered themselves. In the finality the success of the survey was in the hands of the civil administration; the district commissioners and staff.

The strategy for carrying out a leprosy survey depends in the main upon the past experience of the person in overall control. This knowledge can then be adapted to the current situation - such as the non-compliance of Zanzibari women - together with accessibility to the people, consideration of customs etc so that, in the finality, necessary allowances can be made in the results for unavoidable discrepancies.

Ross Innes formed the people into long lines for examination. After they had removed their long gowns, or shirts, they were told

1. Group Zanzibar Town

2. Tea – Zanzibari fashion

3. Group Zanzibar
Ross Innes (rear left) self (rear right)

4. Embarking for Tumbatu
Ross Innes (left foreground) Dr Young (right)

5. Ross Innes with sun-shade

6. Group Pemba
(rear row from left) Polish Doctor, Self, Dr Jones, Ross Innes

7. Group Pemba
(front row from left) Polish Doctor, D.C., Self, Ross Innes

8. Andrea – My assistant/interpreter

9. Polyneuritic patient – deformed hands

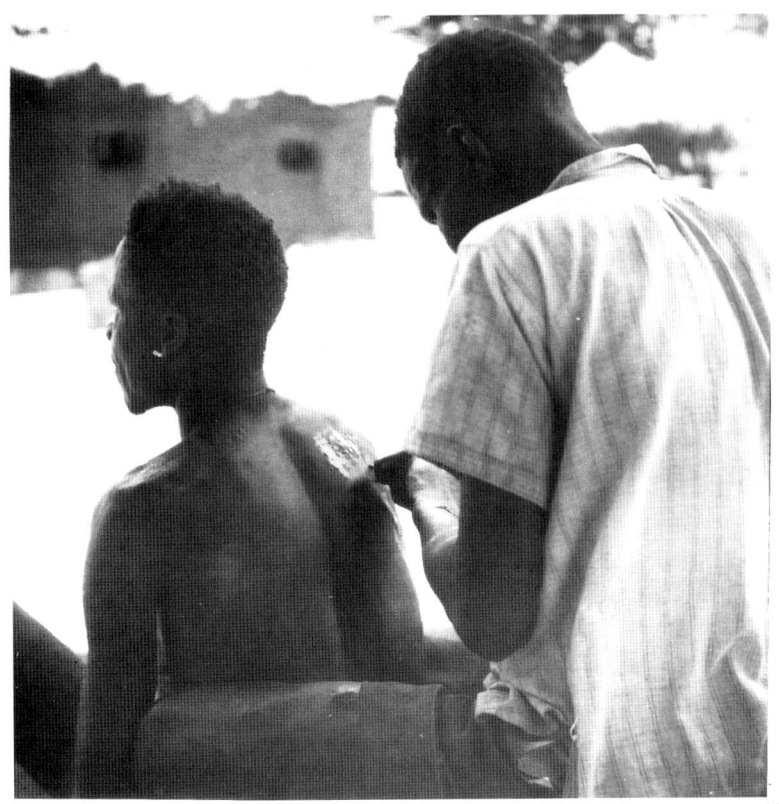

10. Patient having old type of injection with hydnocarpus oil

11. Church – Lui Leprosarium

12. Elase

13. Schoolboys harvesting Ground Nuts

14. Scene near Lui

15. Nile at Juba

16. Juba Ferry

17. Adult grave

18. Chief's grave

19. Hunter's grave

20. Child's grave

21. Leprosy village – Luri Rokwe

22. Elase and Colony Scouts – Lui. Guard of Honour at Wedding

to raise their hands above their heads, palms to the front, while the doctor walked slowly down the line making a visual examination of their skin. This completed, the line was about-faced and the process repeated as before and backs in turn were inspected. The whole proceeding was carried out in the full light of the sun, for this simplified recognition of symptomatic skin changes. If a case was found Ross Innes noted details of the person's name, type of leprosy, age, marital status, number of children and village of origin.

At the beginning I made many a diagnostical error, finding it difficult to distinguish between leprosy and common skin infections, or abnormalities. In case of doubt only laboratory tests could prove or disprove the matter. Little by little, with Ross Innes' patient help, I came to recognise the coppery tinge in the skin of the Negro and the purplish-pink in that of the Arab.

There are distinct differences between the various types of leprosy. Simply they are:

Lepromatus -	causing thickening of the skin, with macules and nodules, giving a leonine appearance to the features.
Tuberculoid -	lesions are in the form of patches, with an outer raised edge. Similar in appearance to the underside of a saucer.
Polyneuritic -	where the nerves are affected. In this type hands and feet are noticeably so. Hands become clawed and fingers and toes may be lost. They do not, as is popularly supposed, just drop off. The

disability is due to the shrinkage of tissue and bone, or is the consequence of an unnoticed injury.

Indeterminate - Where early lesions cannot be identified as a particular type without laboratory tests.

The Lepromatus type was symbolised by the letter	Ll, L2, L3
The Tuberculoid	TI, T2, T3
The Polyneuritic	P1, P2, P3
The Indeterminate as	Im

The numerals after the letters indicate whether the condition be slight, more advanced or very advanced.

Excellent tarmac roads enabled us to reach most localities by car - sometimes walking short distances. Boredom crept in at times, when things were going a little slow, or the numbers presenting themselves for examination were few. This, of course, was inevitable for in common with most research, dreary routine has to be undertaken before a final picture emerges. Not long into the survey Ross Innes asked me if I had travelled this way before and seemed surprised when I replied in the negative. Exclaiming, "Well, you seem to be taking this all very calmly." I did not tell him that my apparent imperturbability was due to a reluctance to make a fool of myself. I wanted to speak from the confidence of experience before I became more voluble. Until then I was content to look, listen and learn.

Visiting the rural areas gave another perspective to Zanzibari life. The tourist, doing a fast trip around the island by taxi saw, often superficially, the novelty of strange peoples and their customs, then departed with souvenirs and sunny memories. They were oblivious to the living conditions in the remoter areas and the breeding grounds for disease, where it was not uncommon to see the sores of yaws on the bodies of children. Sometimes the lesions appeared similar to Tuberculoid lesions of leprosy, but Ross Innes pointed out that if there was a twin sore on the opposite side of the body then it was most likely to be yaws, as leprosy seldom showed this characteristic.

The prevalence of yaws was unnecessary for a course of penicillin would have cured the condition. Theoretically, small dispensaries, with trained medical assistants in charge, could have done much to alleviate this and other problems at source. It would forestall the excuses of those who were unable, or too lazy, to seek treatment and who, by remaining in their home and village, infected others. Very often men came forward asking for treatment for hookworm and were told to go to the hospital. Once we were confronted with a case of Elephantiasis of the scrotum, which was enlarged to the size of a pumpkin and where, from a small mound of foreskin, a dribble of urine trickled down. Caused by the filaria parasitic worm which blocks the lymphatic glands and little or nothing could be done for the condition.

We were about to examine one old man, when he started pleading with Ross Innes to examine him privately. When asked why he explained that a public display of his body would shame him in front of his wives. And, more sadly, as we were about to examine another man a small group nearby started jeering. Ross Innes took a quick look at the examinee's loins and almost immediately told him to cover himself up. Obviously there was something unusual. As Ross Innes began striding away I caught up with him and asked what had been so different about the last man examined. He turned his head and quickly and quietly said, "Hermaphrodite". I dropped back to let the significance of this sink in. A quick glance showed the unfortunate still being harangued by others. The humiliation the poor devil was experiencing must have persisted throughout his life so far. Made an object of derision by both male and female. It would take a very strong-minded person indeed to befriend him and share the snide remarks of tormentors.

At some villages the headman produced coconuts for our party and, after sweating for an hour or so in the hot sun, milk from the nut made a most welcome and refreshing drink. This was not the rather over-sweet milk obtained from husk-stripped mats seen in England, but from those in which the kernel was yet to be formed. To pick the nuts natives bind their ankles together with cords, leaving enough slack to enable them to grip the sides of the tree with the insides of their feet. They ascend the palm's smooth trunk by first clamping the feet and then reaching upwards with the arms. Ross Innes pointed out to me the tell-tale occupational marks of the nut-gatherers, hard, roughened skin on the inside of the feet and chests, caused by the abrasive action against the trunks. A heavy knife was carried in their loincloth and this was used to cut off the coconuts. To prepare for drinking the green nut was held between the feet and, with a knife held in both hands, the nut-gatherer pared away the husk at the top end. The end was then sliced off, leaving a small aperture for drinking. Ross Innes quaffed his drink with great gusto. Lacking his confidence, I lip-paddled around the edge of the shell, with a resultant dribbling of liquid down my shirt and over my shorts. The wet marks on the front of my khaki shorts were an embarrassment until they dried out.

The Arab District Commissioner, who had accompanied Ross Innes and myself on one of our forays, took us to his shamba and proudly showed us the small house built there. Here we rested and had lunch. Later, while Ross Innes had a short siesta, we walked to the nearby beach. A scattered group of women were working away, pounding at something or other with stones. We stopped short of where they were working and the D.C. explained that the women had previously buried coconut husks in the sand and now that they had been softened by the sea-water, they were dug up and pounded to separate the husk's long fibrous strands. When this process was completed the strands would be used in the manufacture of coconut matting, or ropes. The pith of the nut, the copra, had oil extracted from it and the inner hard shell could be used as fuel. In effect nothing was wasted. The climate of Zanzibar was such that crops were produced continuously throughout the year and harvested four times during that period. I walked closer to get a better view of the proceedings but the women resented the intrusion and silently objected by simply walking away.

We continued along the beach and came across pieces of pumice stone scattered over the sand, like so many crouching, grey mice. The D.C. suggested that this had probably come ashore from the wreck of an old Persian trading ship, many of whom had come to grief over the years on the outlying reef. Not far from the cricket ground and golf course a coral reef extended out to sea. A narrow ridge, exposed at ebb tide, could be walked over with suitable stout-soled footwear. Beneath the jagged surface a myriad collection of creatures lurked among the innumerable nooks and crannies. The sea-slug, unmoving, contrasted with the sea-anemone's long-armed mistiness, constantly mobile in the water's gentle flow.

My interest in the reef was aroused after seeing the collection of shells in the Zanzibar Museum. On display were exquisitely small, finely patterned and formed shells, up to the large vari-coloured conch - used in many parts of the island to call people together. The most sought after shells were found on the outer reef. This necessitated diving so I had to be satisfied with what I found on the beach, should the previously mentioned reef be under water. Shells worthy of keeping I stored in round cigarette tins, intending to boil them out later at the first opportunity. The first opportunity was delayed for several weeks, due to forgetfulness on my part and our going to Pemba. Upon return from the latter I opened one of the tins, the stench was abominable. I hurriedly replaced the lid for the smell was beginning to permeate the whole house. What I had there, without a doubt, was the olfactory equivalent of Pandora's Box. Sneaking the tins out of the house I surreptitiously buried them in the small garden. Where, in all probability, they still remain, though much mellowed with age.

Dr Aboud, the only African doctor on the island, had been recruited into the Zanzibar Medical Service from the mainland. He was, in a way, an odd man out and I got the impression that he was not completely accepted socially by European, or Arab. I spoke to him one day of the craftsmanship involved in the making of the large, wooden doors set solidly into the arched doorways of the buildings. The elaborately carved lintels were really magnificent.

Not so many years before many of such doors had been removed from their native settings, to the financial satisfaction of local home owners and the fanciful speculation of Americans. Fortunately, for Zanzibari heritage, the Government had stepped in to curtail the practice before total decimation took place. Dr Aboud took me to an old house in the native quarter where, on a carpenter's trestle-bench at the side of the road, several young men were busily carving lintels. The design was only roughly indicated upon the wood, but the completed work was very fine. The finished doors and their surrounding have intricate patterns, in which old devices are retained. Such as the fish emblem at the bottom of a doorpost, representing the Egyptian Fish God; the sea waves climbing upwards represented the Arab merchant's livelihood and entwined lotus flowers - hopefully - fertility. The face of the doors was studded with various sized, conical brass nail-heads. The greater the wealth and social position of the house's owner, the larger and more elaborately carved the door.

Some days, when I wanted to be alone, I went to the beach; to lie back upon the form embracing comfort of the sun-warmed sand. To lazily watch native fishermen push out their out-rigger canoes, from calm, inshore waters, to where white-capped waves marked the line of potentially dangerous coral. Then their gentle bobbing progress before finding the gap in the reef and entering the comparative safety of rougher water. At times a soft blurring of sea and sky made everything appear as one and you drifted into a sense of peace. A time also to think of my trunk, containing camp-bed, mosquito-net etc. taken to the mainland in error and not yet returned.

Chapter 6

It appeared to start with a needle stuck in a cow. A hypodermic needle containing serum to inoculate against anthrax. But this was not the underlying cause of the trouble; just the catalyst needed to bring to a head the political and religious resentment of many years. Once the pot began to boil then opportunist agitators seized upon the unpopular civic edict of cattle inoculation for their own ends.

Against traditional practice there had been, over the past years, restrictions upon the movement of cattle. A new air-strip had meant grazing land commandeered, while new roads and European housing had also meant loss of land.

The Government Veterinary Officer, an Irishman, went to the area of Kiembe Samaki, in the south-western part of the island, where a few cases of anthrax had been found. This was one of several areas designated as selected points to where cattle could be driven, as a matter of convenience, for inoculation. The cattle owners distrusted the Arab Mudir, who spoke for the Vet. They listened to his words in silence. A silence which continued until both officials had gone. Then voices were raised against the proposed programme. Was it not a fact, it was said, that the white man had given the needle to cattle on the mainland and they had all died? (This was the result of using defective serum supplied from an Egyptian source.) It was a trick to kill their cattle and so free more land for Europeans to build more houses. And so the argument and agitation went on until, at last, it was decided to resist any attempt by the Government to inoculate cattle.

After a few days, resolve weakened and a few cattle-owners

submitted to the Government order. But seventeen remained adamant in their resistance, with the result they were summoned to appear before the Magistrate at Zanzibar Town.

Ross Innes and I were not conversant with the situation until we visited the Kiembe Samaki area. Instead of being greeted by an expected hundred or so people, there were but a few elderly villagers awaiting us. The headman explained that everyone who was able had gone to Zanzibar Town to attend the trial of their friends the following day.

The day of the trial we were not due to go out on survey until the early afternoon. After a quick lunch at the hotel at mid-day, I was returning to Dr Young's when I encountered, in a side street, about a dozen askari, armed with riot shields and long batons, being briefed by an officer. Entering the square in front of the Courthouse I was surprised to find that the small crowd I had seen earlier had now grown considerably. An Arab A.D.C[*]. I had met on a previous occasion was nearby so I asked him if he thought there might be trouble. When he confirmed that this was so, I thought it prudent to get indoors as quickly as possible. The Young's house, being near, I hurried towards it, pausing at the door to survey the scene once more. The A.D.C. was now attempting to make himself heard above the ever increasing hubbub of the crowd as he read them the Riot Act. It was a mixed crowd; some there because they were curious, others friends of those on trial and, more significantly, as was reported later, a small nucleus of trouble-makers. The latter could be observed gathering about them small groups of people to instil in them thoughts of outrage, real

---

[*] Assistant District Commissioner

and imagined, of any slight or wrong in the past. To a large extent they succeeded in their aims. For the crowd to become a cohesive force all they needed was a common purpose; a cause around which to rally.

The door of Dr Young's house was shut. I hammered upon it ineffectively with my fist. The door felt as rigid and immoveable as stone. Behind me the crowd appeared more restless and vociferous. I struck the door again and again and gave a shout, taking a chance on attracting the crowd's attention. At last, to my relief, Ahmed, the Young's cook, opened the door just wide enough for me to slip inside. The family were upstairs and Dr Young told Ahmed to take the two children to their bedroom and remain with them. He also passed on a message from Dr Tallack that because of the situation outside, the survey programme would be delayed until things had settled down. Not having experienced this type of occurrence before, at one stage I went to one of the windows to take photographs of the scene below. But Dr Young told me bluntly not to show myself, otherwise it might provoke the crowd and attract a volley of stones. I saw the sense of this and compromised by standing back to look upon a more restrictive view of the proceedings. It was tempting to take a closer look, especially when a palm tree at the side of the house suddenly started swaying to and fro, as if in a gale. From the shouts below we conjectured that lower branches were being ripped off for use against the police. However, a fair view was obtainable from the windows, for they were rectangular apertures in which were set vertically, several iron bars about six inches apart.

A police van drew up at the Courthouse entrance. Not far

away, to the side, two fire pumps were strategically positioned, ready for use if required. The windows and side windows of the van were reinforced with wire-mesh, while the bodywork had been extended upwards in the form of a cage with strong, steel netting. Warning was given from inside the building that prisoners were being brought out. There was no doubt of their guilt and the trial, in effect, had merely taken place to impose sentences upon the law-breakers.

The clamorous crowd surged forward, anticipating the prisoners' exit, waving sticks; some wore sandals wrapped around their fists as weapons. The police, a thin khaki line of authority, were forced back to the Courthouse wall. Stones and other missiles rained down upon them and, when they lifted their shields to protect their heads, some of the crowd ran in close and belaboured their feet and legs. The askari appeared to be under an order of restraint, but offered enough resistance to allow some of the prisoners into the rear of the van. A lone figure appeared on the Courthouse roof, flung up his arms, as if in prayer, and cried, "It's Holy War, what are you waiting for?" This simple and direct declaration increased any religions fervour of the crowd.

Would-be rescuers swarmed over the van, beating at it with sticks and stones. Headlights disintegrated, windows crazed over, making it near impossible for the driver to see his way. Those at the rear of the van came under powerful jets of water from the fire-pumps and were picked off like so many rag dolls, to lie wet, winded and bedraggled on the ground. The driver was attempting to get away in spite of the many rioters clinging to the bonnet and cab of the van. Slowly it started off along the road leading out of town, to be eventually lost to our restrictive view. At its going the crowd began to disperse, many making their way to the prison, where another crowd awaited the van's arrival.

Soon afterwards, our survey party slunk out of town, with one eye on the road, the other open for trouble. In the rural area the atmosphere was different altogether, with no sign of agitation or resentment shown by those we visited. Things appeared quite normal, with the occasional native sidling up to Ross Innes asking for a note to take to hospital for some vague complaint, or a reliable remedy for the enquirer's impotency. Speculating upon the earlier events of the day, we naturally wondered if there had been further developments. On stopping at Walezo Mission Station, where there happened to be a telephone, an urgent message awaited us. All doctors were requested to report back to town immediately. Things had taken a serious turn since our departure.

The police van we had seen zigzagging down the road from the Courthouse had not travelled any great distance before it was made to crash into a wall. In the resulting confusion the prisoners were released by the people clinging to the outside of the van. However, another van, similar to the first, had left from the rear of the Courthouse when the riotous disturbance was in full swing at the front. This van was halted near the vicinity of the prison by the crowd there. The European police officer went into the crowd to plead with the crowd to let the van through. To no avail - his personal confrontation nearly cost him his life. He was grabbed by the testicles and wrestled to the ground. An askari sergeant, in charge of a rifle squad on the prison wall saw what had happened and then, when he heard shouts of "Kill him" - followed by the passing of a knife through the crowd, he gave orders to open fire. Five people were killed and at least twice that number wounded before the crowd scattered, leaving their intended victim lying senseless on the ground.

That evening, Europeans in out-lying districts were advised to bring their families into town as a precaution against retaliation for what had occurred. A special constabulary was formed among the Europeans. Each man was given a steel helmet, rifle and ammunition. The night passed uneventfully and when the next day dawned, the sun beamed down upon a situation which, for the moment at least, appeared to be far less explosive.

Tumbatu Island lies off the north-west coast of Zanzibar and is one of the larger off-shore islands. The village of Mkokotoni faced Tumbatu across a three mile stretch of dappled sea; blues and greens rivalled one another for varying richness and intensity of colour. All controlled by the distance of coral from the surface of the sea. Here was coral playing Beauty - while at other times in destructive role, it played the Beast.

The village was a fishing community and several roughly-hewn canoes were pulled up on the beach; others lay at anchor off-shore. We had visited Mkokotoni on a previous occasion and were surprised to see a giant Galapagos tortoise sauntering down the path to the village. Ross Innes, ever ready to use his new camera, took my photograph supposedly riding on the creature's back. It was so large I could barely straddle it. How the tortoise came to be in Zanzibar was something of a mystery. Locals said it had always been there. It is safe to assume it was brought there by an early trader, but for what purpose remains unknown. Dotted along the beach were roughly constructed shelters, beneath which hung gutted fish, together with several small octopus. Standing back from the beach on rising ground was the large, spacious Government resthouse, little used, except by an established clientele of lizards and spiders.

Because of the inshore shallows we were obliged to wade out to the dhow which was taking us to Tumbatu. Ross Innes added an individual touch to the scene by pushing off seawards, holding up his shorts with one hand and a large umbrella with the other.

It was a pleasant crossing. The creak of oars. A soft breeze encouraging a gentle flapping of the large white sail, was an inducement to sleep. A tendency further aided by the sun-glint off the sea, which periodically closed your eyes. Entirely relaxed, I but vaguely heard Doctors Ross Innes and Young in conversation with the Arab D.C.[*] and his brother, who were accompanying us that day.

Reaching Tumbatu at last, after a necessarily erratic course to avoid parts of the reef, we grounded just short of the beach and waded ashore. We were supposed to have been met by the headman. There was no sign of him, which allowed time to inspect the innumerable multi-tinted, small shells lying around between widely scattered clumps of green-black, half-dried seaweed. From a group of tall palms a flight of small, yellow birds winged upwards, in ever-changing patterns, against the clear blue sky. A monkey chattered at us from cover of a rock cluster. The spell was broken by the arrival of the headman. After the usual greetings, he said he would return to the nearby village and bring his people to

---

[*] District Commissioner

us. They were disappointingly few in number, but were all the headman said he could produce. There was nothing for it but to sail to the far end of the island, where the majority of the people lived.

Keeping close inshore, to avoid the coral, we eventually rounded a small headland and entered the bay beyond. White-robed figures lined the beach-top in a compact mass, like icing on a cake. Our spirits rose. Our day was not to be wasted after all. But as we drew closer it was noticeable that the crowd, for the most part, consisted of young men. We did not think to compare this situation with that outside the Courthouse during the riot earlier in the week. Like then, women and children were not on view and we naively assumed they had gathered elsewhere to be examined.

Our progress ashore was watched in ominous silence. When asked to line up for examination, the young men protested with a vehemence that was frightening. They came up close to us, shouting in our faces and making threatening gestures with their fists. Their features distorted by self generated anger and hate. I became a little isolated from the rest of the party and, when lighting a cigarette to steady my nerves, noticed my hand was trembling slightly. I was scared. It was one thing to view a riot from a window, quite another to be personally involved. Meanwhile, the Arab D.C. was trying, unsuccessfully, to ascertain the reason for our adverse reception. But the crowd declined to give a logical reason for their behaviour, just expressed a continuing determination not to co-operate.

When some of the older men elected to be examined and fell into line, the younger men forcibly removed them and several scuffles developed. One man was thrown into the sea by members of the crowd, to gamely return to shore raining blows and seawater. The A.D.C. went to his rescue and became involved in the general melee. As he was over six feet tall and weighed about seventeen stone, he gave a good account of himself before his elder brother, the D.C. extricated him from the fray. And, by so doing, no doubt prevented the brawl extending to other members of our party. Amid sardonic jeers we left the beach - relieved to be able to do so. For awhile we sat in the headman's hut and drank coffee, while the D.C. once more attempted to pacify the people. To no avail. We waded out to the dhow, climbed aboard and set sail for Mkokotoni, taking with us the man who had been thrown into the sea; partly for his own safety and as a witness to what had occurred.

The incident had visibly shaken the D.C. and he could offer no adequate explanation for what had happened. From a survey point of view it had been a complete waste of time. The more frustrating because examination of Tumbatu people, during our earlier Zanzibar examinations, had indicated a possible high incidence of leprosy on Tumbatu. Several speculative interpretations were given for our reception. The first was that due to the isolation of the island and the D.C.'s infrequent visits, civil control had been unknowingly lost. Alternatively, the Tumbatu people had seen our survey as the first of many incursions upon their way of life - which included a fair bit of smuggling around the coast.

A more colourful theory offered by the European residents, was that Tumbatu was a training school for witchcraft, drawing its initiates from the African mainland. But the theory expounded by

Ross Innes and one which, I must confess I privately ridiculed at the time as 'Reds under the bed', placed the cause at the feet of Communist agitators who, he said, had been active on the mainland for some time.

I am now convinced Ross Innes' explanation was the true one. Not many years after our visit a Communist inspired coup brought about a racial blood-bath in which hundreds of Arabs and others were killed. The island of Tumbatu was the centre for this uprising and perhaps our visit had, unknown to us, proved to be an inconvenient intrusion at the time.

The day following this unhappy occurrence we visited two small villages in the vicinity of Mkokotoni. As the inhabitants were kinsfolk of the people of Tumbatu, we half expected trouble of some kind. We were right in our analysis. At the first village the villagers refused to be examined and Ross Innes noticed several ringleaders from the Tumbatu confrontation among the crowd. Dropping a soft word here - a heavy hand there. The D.C. could do little else but appeal to them to consider their decision while we visited the other village on our itinerary.

The second village was deserted when we arrived. Ross Innes and I waited in the shade of the headman's house while the D.C. went to look for its missing occupier. The day was hot and, at ground level, appeared windless, until you became aware of the rustle of the high palm-tops swaying darkly overhead against the sky. I contemplated the nuts and thought thirstily of their cool contents.

The D.C. returned with the headman and news that the men of the village were down at the mosque, a short distance away near the beach. It was approached by a sandy, much foot-printed path, which wound through slim, grey-trunked palms. As we neared the mosque, the men came out of the building, chanting and waving long sticks. We asked the D.C. what it was all about. In no way was this a welcoming committee. With a worried expression on his face he said they had been praying for victory. Over whom? Why - us! The situation seemed unreal; over dramatic. Ross Innes did not entirely accept the D.C.'s interpretation of the position.

I walked with him towards the group who were jigging about in a semi-circle. There was an immediate reaction to our approach and threatening glances were flung in our direction, and by the aggressive waving of their lethal-looking sticks they would as soon have thrown them as well.

Every few seconds one of the dancers leapt into the air with a yell. My nerves jumped with him. I was relieved when Ross Innes decided that this might be the time to retrace our steps. At a safe distance we turned to see the villagers marching back into the mosque to give thanks for their victory.

Arriving back at the first village we found no change in attitude. The last few days of the Zanzibar survey had been a disaster. Would we get a similar reaction in Pemba? It was decided to take the risk and go as planned.

My trunk had still not been returned from the mainland.

Chapter 7

Tourists were rarely seen on Pemba because of the scarcity of transport and lack of accommodation. Visitors, usually employed by the Government, were invariably lodged with European residents living in their Government provided homes.

The only steamer making a regular weekly voyage to Pemba was the 'Al-Said'. We boarded her late one Thursday afternoon, forcing our way through an excited dockside crowd, gathered to view the steamer's departure. The lower, open deck was crammed with native passengers and we were obliged to high-step our way over their sprawling bodies and assorted baggage. We eventually reached the short flight of steps leading to the upper, first-class accommodation and saw our luggage into the cabin.

After supper, we spent an hour on deck enjoying the sea breezes and delaying having to enter the heated atmosphere of our cabin. It was on the small side for two to share comfortably and neither the small port-hole nor the electric fan did much to relieve the humidity. Ross Innes went to the bath-cabin first. Upon his return he indicated a bath was being poured for me. Upon taking but one step into the bath-cabin I was confronted with a blanket of steam. Further into the murk I could make out the vague shape of the steward. Then my glasses steamed over and I remained where I was, reluctant to enter an encompassment of unknown hazards. From where I stood I asked the Zanzibari steward to add cold water to the bath.

"Yes sir," came the reply, somewhat muffled by the heavy atmosphere. The steam became thicker and I realised more hot water was being put into the bath. I made my way to the steward's dim shape and, indicating what appeared to be superheated steam coming out of the tap, said exasperatedly, "cold water - COLD water."

"Yes," he agreed with a beatific smile, indicating the scalding steam. There was a language problem here. I made him turn the water off before the cabin was flooded. After he left I looked around for a safe place to put my spectacles, concerned that should I put them down the atmosphere, combined with myopia, would prevent my finding them again. I wiped them wetly and sat down on the edge of the bath to consider the situation; careful not to introduce my body into the water so that it became parboiled. To have cooled the water down sufficiently to bathe would have taken more water than the bath would hold. In the meantime I stripped off, now and then hopefully testing the water's temperature, while perspiration dripped from me like fat from a barbecued sausage. At last I was forced to give up the idea of a bath and had to be satisfied with a hot wipe all over before returning to the cabin.

Ross Innes looked up from the book he was reading. "You look hot." he commented.

I told him what had happened - the difficulty with the language - and he chuckled his way to sleep. It was hours before I cooled down sufficiently to get to sleep myself. Now, looking back, I wonder whether Ross Innes had told the bath-steward that I liked a hot bath. The doctor had a wicked sense of humour at times.

The following morning we awoke to find the 'Al-Said' anchored off-shore from the Pemba town of Wete. After breakfast on board we were taken by launch to the wooden jetty, where we were greeted by Dr Jones, who was in charge of Wete Hospital. A young, slightly built Welshman, with a rather worried expression, probably caused by the intrusion of two strangers upon his bachelorhood. From the jetty he pointed out his house, on the brow of a rise overlooking the bay.

Ross Innes was accommodated in an upper room of the doctor's house, while I was given a bed in the unoccupied European ward, a small annexe some fifty yards from the house. This suited me very well for I welcomed the privacy. I grew to relish the view each morning as I went to the house for breakfast. If early, I walked to the edge of the rise to look out over the bay, where small, native craft snuggled up to the shoreline, as if asleep. And too, the ever delightful pleasure of watching colourful humming birds, wings whirring away, as they hung in space deep-tonguing the flowers in the garden.

As we did not have to begin the Pemba survey until the Monday following our arrival, we had several days in which to familiarise ourselves with the immediate locality. Dr Jones had mentioned in conversation that an old summer-house, adjacent to a small vegetable garden, was in danger of collapse. The wooden supports had been weakened by the voracious activities of white ants. He thought, for safety, it should be demolished.

I suppose most of us like to take part in approved demolition, so we willingly agreed to do the job for him. Just one good shove and the structure was down. While carrying the debris to a proposed site for a fire, there was a moment of panic when a rather belligerent snake dropped out of the thatch. In answer to a summoning call from Dr Jones, the cook came running bearing a large meat-knife in his fist. With a wild swipe he cut the snake in two, producing a phenomena of the snake's head, plus but a few inches of body, rearing up defiantly, ready to strike. A direct blow on the head dispatched it. We took no further chances and burnt the rest of the debris where it lay.

A narrow, dirt road left the doctor's garden and passed the hospital buildings, before joining the main street of the town. On our first and only excursion to the shopping centre Ross Innes bought himself a pipe and tobacco "To keep away the flies and kill some of the smells." I picked out a cheap fibre suitcase for future use. A false economy, in a way, but my resources did not permit greater extravagance. We visited the shops at night, when the only lighting was that from hurricane lamps, hook-hung at the shop-fronts. Restricted viewing gave the locality the character of a shanty town; the shops' general shabbiness contrasting strongly with the wide variety of gaudy merchandise strung about the open-fronted verandas.

On the opposite side of the bay stood the Arab-styled, two storied house of the European District Commissioner, wife and two children. The young boy had travelled over with us on the steamer from Zanzibar, to spend his school holidays with his parents and sister. When Ross Innes and I had lunch there, the Sunday after our arrival, we were invited to a combined fishing and swimming excursion to one of the small beaches, where it was intended we should picnic. During the discussion of arrangements the subject of the Stone-fish came up, it being not uncommon in the area. Camouflaged among scattered stones on the sea-bed and sometimes half-hidden in the sand, the danger lay in the line of needle-sharp spikes along its spine. Should you be unfortunate enough to step on the fish the poison not only caused the foot to swell up like a balloon, but the victim also suffered acute, excruciating pain.

On the day of the excursion we boarded a launch at the jetty. There were nine of us in the party; the D.C. and his family, Drs Ross Innes and Jones, two nursing sisters - one of whom was stationed at Chake Chake - and myself. The two nurses for some reason did not appear particularly affable. We slowly chugged out to sea with lines thrown out, but had no success with our fishing before we arrived at the small beach. Here the sea was a large open pool, contained at one end by the sand and on two other sides by thick mangrove. We swam without mishap and there was, perhaps, more danger from the sharp-pointed mangrove shoots barely protruding through the sand, than Stone-fish.

As the tide receded from the mangroves, leaving small pools of water in the sandy mud, out of the corner of my eye I saw a movement in one of the pools. Outgoing circular ripples betrayed the position of a Mud-hopper. At first I had no idea what it was for just part of the large head and protruding eyes were visible. I moved towards it. To my surprise the fish, for that's what it was, jumped away across the mud to safety, propelled by its large flipper-like fins lying just behind the head.

I then made out others in the vicinity and would have stayed watching their antics, but was called away for our return. These were the only fish we saw throughout the day as nothing was caught on the way home.

To me, an inveterate beachcomber, the tide-lines of Pemba, like Zanzibar, projected an aura of expectant discovery as they drew me to them. On a beach, not far from Wete, Persian beads had been found, similar to those found on the northern beaches of Zanzibar. Pieces of pottery were also deposited on shore from time to time. Both pottery and beads were said to originate from an old Persian trading depot, now inundated by the sea. Zanzibar was probably first settled by Persians about A.D. 700 and the oldest remaining building of Persian origin on that island is a mosque, dating from A.D. 1107. On Tumbatu Island are the remains of an old Shirazian (Persian) city and the island's inhabitants - the Watumbatu - are said to be of Persian descent. The people of Pemba also have a fair mixture of Persian blood. There had also been a Portuguese influence upon the islands, in the earlier part of the 20th century, and the Portuguese sport of Bull-baiting, as distinct from bull-killing, was still a part of Pemba life.

A few miles from Wete, at Makondeni, was the small Government leprosy colony in the charge of a native assistant. The colony had been established for a number of years, but lack of real interest in the welfare of the occupants had denied the patients adequate treatment. When first established, the colony was merely a refuge for those suffering from leprosy; a place where they were guaranteed food, shelter and isolation. The colony was much in need of development, both in building and treatment. The site itself appeared to be ideally situated on two sections of high ground. A small spring, rising on the lower level, supplied the colony with water all the year round. A year or so after our survey, this colony came under the auspices of BELRA, with one of their workers permanently resident there.

A subtle change had taken place in my attitude towards leprosy, during the Zanzibar survey and, in particular, towards those suffering from the disease. My initial abhorrence had been replaced by a more clinical approach during examinations, yet there was time now for sympathy, instead of revulsion. In one of the huts at Makondeni we found a young girl of twenty with her husband, who was a few years older. A beautiful girl who could still smile in spite of the polyneuritic deformities of hands and feet. To see someone near to my own age in such a condition made the 'hardships' I had previously experienced in my life fade into insignificance, when compared with this young girl's future. I felt myself giving way to emotion and had to turn aside until I had recovered my composure. It might be argued that sympathy is not enough, unless backed with practical help. This is undoubtedly true but, in the beginning, one must care and this in itself brings hope to those in need.

The reticence and subsequent non-cooperation of the women of Zanzibar was in direct contrast to the unanimity shown by the women of Pemba. Our reception on the small island of Mbali, just off the north coast of Pemba, was a notable exception, to say the least. The European D.C. escorting us casually mentioned, as background information, that the inhabitants rarely saw a white man, apart from himself, so that our visit would be something of a novelty for the islanders. Life on the island tended to be rather primitive; water for drinking purposes was dependent upon rainfall and what could be channelled, via large banana-tree leaves, into pots for storage. The purpose of the D.C.'s own visit was to inspect the progress of the construction of a large storage tank, for the peoples' needs, while we were otherwise engaged.

The first thing that struck us as we went ashore was the large number of children. ("They have nothing else to do, y'know." a Zanzibar resident confided.) It was the children who came to greet us first, pulling our canoe onto the shore. We were then scrutinised with undisguised curiosity. The usual explanation for the reason of our visit was given and then we examined the men near the shore.

The women and girls awaited us in the village, a short distance away. We went through our normal procedure of placing them in lines but found, upon turning our backs, that they broke ranks and surrounded us as we were jotting down our findings. The D.C.'s hint concerning the rarity of European visits was made clear when we were individually surrounded by young girls. The examination we had planned turned into a fiasco as we ourselves were examined; when dark skinned hands explored white-skinned legs and thighs inside our shorts. I glanced around at innocent-looking, smiling faces, whose owners had, shortly before, been tugging at my body hair. The older women stood back, holding themselves with glee as they enjoyed the spectacle of us twisting and turning to avoid the girls' sometimes intimate explorations. I feared the adults might be tempted to urge their off-spring on to more embarrassing possibilities. Were we about to be publicly de-bagged? Would I be forced to lie back and think of England? I glanced across to where Ross Innes appeared to be doing a half-hearted highland fling, with little girls ringed around his loins like a kilt. There was obviously no concession to age.

I caught his rather desperate eye above the bobbing heads. "Get a rough estimate of how many, Vear." he shouted, still in control of his faculties, if nothing else. "I think we'd better leave."

So we withdrew, trying to preserve our dignity against a

background of ringing laughter from the motley crowd of females, whose feelings for us had been more physical than abstract. But we put on a brave face and tried to look as though it was all in a day's work. The D.C. greeted our arrival back at the water storage project with an enquiring look of amusement, obviously having suffered a similar fate in the past.

"All right?" he enquired.

"All right." replied Ross Innes. A little sourly, I thought.

There was no mention of this in the doctor's final report on the survey. A pity, it would have livened it up.

Due to the complaisant attitude of the people the Pemba survey was much more congenial for us than that of Zanzibar. For one thing we had the antics of the island Fat Man, who loomed large in our examinations. He had taken it upon himself to see how many times he could fool us into giving him an examination. We decided to play along with him - it made a small diversion anyway - while he enjoyed the apparent success of his 'deception'. We wondered where he would pop up next and began to look out for him. In all, we must have 'examined' him some half a dozen times. After each examination he would rush off to his friends in great glee.

In contrast to this happy-go-lucky extrovert were people who, knowing they had leprosy, tried to conceal it. A slight turning away of the body, the wearing of shoes, in lieu of sandals, to hide deformities of the feet. Though, as hands as well as feet are often affected at the same time, tell-tale signs on the hands made the wearing of shoes more suspect. Sometimes a turban, or hat, would be pushed forward on the head to cover a patch on the forehead, or backwards to cover a patch on the neck. With the lack of facilities for leprosy treatment at the time, together with isolation in a colony, it was understandable that some should seek to hide signs of the disease. On the odd occasion scarified parts of the body suggested a form of native treatment of leprosy. Was this effective? Sometimes the disease was arrested and did not spread further, but usually there was but a temporary respite.

Chake Chake, once of major importance, but now superseded by Wete as Pemba's centre of administration, showed some of the glory of its past with huge old Arab houses on a rise overlooking the bay. A similar siting to that of Wete. But, in addition to these, there was an old Portuguese fort overlooking a mangrove creek and now used as a police station.

We made an early visit to the hospital, under the charge of a Polish doctor who had barely survived one of the German concentration camps. We were told that, as yet, he had not fully recovered from the experience. Other staff at the hospital were the nursing sister from Yorkshire, who had been on the picnic with us, and local recruits. We toured the wards and Ross Innes, upon examining the patients, discovered one man being treated for a fractured leg who had leprosy as well. The resident doctor was surprised and the sister, probably recalling the very worst she had heard concerning leprosy, was visibly disturbed and wanted to know what they should do to isolate the patient. Ross Innes explained that as the case was of the mild tubercular type, the chance of cross-infection was remote, providing normal prophylactic procedures were adopted.

Her consternation was not uncommon at first experiencing leprosy. My own experience at Walezo confirmed that, but the shock she felt must have been greater than mine, because the sighting was unexpected. This, in addition to her having no medical knowledge whatsoever of the disease, as she confessed.

There has been a dread of leprosy since before Biblical times and, of course, there are several references to lepers in the bible itself. But casual allusion does not bear on the memory as do descriptions of an unkempt, lurching figure prowling the streets and highways with a bell and a chant of 'Unclean'. Leprosy was once rife in the British Isles and the record of its past infiltration lies in ancient leper hospitals, usually established and run by a religious order, and leper squints in old churches. A disease of overcrowding and close personal contact, it has reason to be less feared than Aids, for leprosy can be cured.

After lunch at the doctor's house we went out to examine the population of Chake Chake. Everything went off smoothly and we gave our Fat Man his usual examination. We were standing talking when suddenly Ross Innes said, "Get over there Vear and I'll take your photograph."

I mentally preened myself and stood where he had indicated.

He looked down at the focusing screen. "Back a bit." he murmured. "Now back a little more."

I moved back and found myself in the lower branches of a bushy shrub. The next minute I was beating frantically at my head and shoulders to dislodge the dozens of ants I had dislodged from their perch and who were venting their annoyance on my person.

"What's up?" enquired Ross Innes, with pseudo-innocence, still going through the motions of composing a picture of my antics.

"Ants." I grunted, disgruntled and slapping away at my

tormentors. "You want to be careful with those." smiled the doctor. "They bite."

It was now obvious that he had manoeuvred me into the ants for his own, rotten photographic ends. So I just had to grin and rub it.

The hills of Pemba appeared softer and more rounded than those of Zanzibar, with spacious views across clove and coffee plantations. Here too there was evidence of 'White Death.' Good roads were few and far between so we had more walking to do. The BELRA Secretary, Mr Hoare, had hinted that among other transport mules might be needed in Pemba. We were spared this, but I would have liked to have seen Ross Innes leg-hanging a mule, reins in one hand, large umbrella in the other.

Apart from the usual crops of cloves, chillies, coffee; red-peppers and a limited amount of copra, Pemba also produced a large amount of rice. This was made possible by streams which meandered through the valleys throughout the year. At one such place the water had inundated the road, along which we were walking, and Ross Innes refused to walk through the few inches of water, in case of hookworm. We were carried across on someone's back as they splashed through with bare feet. On our return a passing bullock-cart gave us a fortuitous lift. Near the homesteads were betel-nut palms and the remnants of chewed nut, spat out on the ground, suggested murder most foul. Chewers of the betel-nut were easily identified by their red-stained teeth. When they smiled you wished they hadn't.

A few days before the Pemba survey finished we had a hair-cut. Ross Innes had looked rather pointedly at my unruly hair and suggested it was about time some was cut off; he'd have his cut as well. Thus making us more acceptable in more formal surroundings. Dr Jones arranged for a local barber, an Indian, to come to the house.

He duly arrived, one afternoon, carrying his tools of trade in a cloth bag. Extracting from it scissors, brush, cloth and several pairs of clippers, he arranged them neatly on a small table next to a chair.

Ross Innes had greeted the Indian in some dialect which could have been Hindi, Urdu or Tibetan for all I knew, but it seemed to ring a bell with the barber and the two were soon chatting away quite freely. I stood back, feeling rather out of it as Ross Innes seated himself on the chair and had a cloth tucked around his neck. After a short while the doctor appeared to lose interest in the conversation and the former animated discourse died away. Job completed and brushed down, Ross Innes rose smartly from the chair and waved me towards it for my turn.

The cloth was shaken and placed around my neck. Ross Innes, pipe in mouth, had started talking to the barber once more. The latter, obviously delighted at the involvement, delayed starting to cut my hair for a minute or so. Then, as Ross Innes continued to speak, the barber circled around me, looking, touching, as if planning an assault upon my person.

Conversation ceased for a moment and the Indian came in close to begin. At once I was enveloped in his highly spiced breath, the basis of which still remains one of the mysteries of the Orient. I willed the barber to finish quickly. I even prayed he finish quickly, but such a trivial entreaty was ignored. Ross Innes went on talking, delaying the barber in his work while I sat and suffered near marination by the all-embracing breath.

It was then I realised the reason for Ross Innes' out-of-character reticence to talk at the last stages of his hair-cut. He confessed to me later of his amusement as he watched my facial contortions and the periodic reddening of my face as I held my breath. He had, of course, deliberately delayed the operation. As I mentioned before, he had a wicked sense of humour.

Survey finished, we returned to Zanzibar. Before he left for Nairobi the following day he said, "When you get to Nairobi, look me up. We'll have a meal together." I was sorry to see him go. I would miss his chubby, chuckling face, even though at times I was the cause of it. One moment of cheer though - my trunk had come back from the mainland.

Results of the surveys showed Zanzibar to have an average leprosy rate of 3.9 cases per thousand head of population. The Pemba rate was slightly higher at 5.5 cases per thousand. The incidence was far lower than that on the mainland. My first Sudanese results came as a shock.

Chapter 8

While we were being molested at Mbali, the management of the Zanzibar Hotel had sent out distress signals to the Zanzibar Medical Service concerning me. Due of an oversight on my part I had omitted to let them know I was going to Pemba. My absence at the meal-table had been construed as my having done a bunk - a runner - without paying my dues. This I rectified upon my return to Zanzibar. I was presented with the bill, together with a mass of chits I had signed during my stay. I threw the latter away, much to the chagrin of the BELRA head office in London, when they received the bare bill from me, without a breakdown of its integral parts, so that my indulgences (had there been any) could be scrutinised. And I thought I was doing them a favour by saving on postage.

My journey to the Sudan by steamer and train was booked on my behalf by the Zanzibar Medical Service. I left several days after Ross Innes' departure by air. The first stage of my journey was to Mombasa and the steamer was, appropriately, the 'Mombasa'. It was fundamentally a coastal steamer. A narrow passage-way ran through the accommodation deck, off which were cabins for ship's officers and passengers. The porters carrying my luggage lurched their way to my allotted cabin, ham-acting out their exertions, eyes rolling in my direction to ensure I was fully aware of their Herculean efforts on my behalf. Equity would have applauded their professionalism and the Zanzibar Amateur Dramatic Society welcomed them with open arms - had they been white.

My large trunk, which had to date travelled further than

myself, gave the porters a chance to indulge in their full repertoire of agonised groans and grunts. Facial expressions suggesting their fear of double hernias.

I tipped them for their performance, rather than their porterage, but detected a genuine groan or two when they saw the size of my tip. No doubt they had assumed, because I had been given the doctor's cabin, with the grandiose title of 'Surgery' on the door, that I was good for much more. I don't know where the doctor stowed his gear when he was aboard. There was barely room for me to turn around because of the clutter of luggage. I had to step on my trunk to get into the bunk.

There were two other passengers besides myself. A middle-aged woman stenographer and a red-headed, bushy moustached oil company executive, both of whom were taking up employment in Mombasa. Later that evening, after dinner, we sat together and enjoyed several hours of conversation, swapping experiences. Enjoyment which, upon my part anyhow, was helped by an unaccustomed quantity of 'Tusker' beer. The bottle label, bearing a picture of a posturing elephant, could be taken as an indication of the beer's strength, or its source. Depending upon individual taste, or distaste.

Mombasa is situated upon an island, connected to the mainland by a causeway, and was of importance to Kenya as its only access to the sea. The port also served the inland territories of Rhodesia and Uganda. Somewhat surprisingly, I learnt Mombasa was not part of Kenya, but leased from the Sultan of Zanzibar.

The voyage was short and after we docked the following morning, I had the first of a series of worries over luggage.

Memories of my trunk gave rise to fear of items being misdirected and I determined to keep as many as possible under my care. There appeared to be no set system for transporting my belongings to the Customs, once unloaded from the ship. People were willing to help me, or help themselves, and I had visions of my belongings finding their way into the local shops. Several of the porters wore a sash around their body with the legend 'Free Porter' emblazoned in large black letters upon a scarlet background. Watching their antics I mentally assessed them as 'Free and Easy Porter', as I rather bewilderingly followed their carefree walk and comments to the Customs shed.

Emerging from the clutches of the Customs and the porters, I went into town in a taxi. Through the port gates, under a railway bridge and onto the wide road leading to town. I found a hotel not far from the town centre and convenient to the railway station.

That afternoon, I decided to contact one of the Scots I had travelled with on the outward voyage. He had mentioned that he stayed in a hostel of sorts about three quarters of a mile outside Mombasa. From the edge of town I could make out several buildings in the distance, doing a shimmy in the heat haze. Everything seemed parched and hot. I set off on a well-trodden path heading approximately in the right direction, across the flat, rather desolate looking land, devoid of life. Well almost - striding along well ahead of me was the tall uniformed figure of an askari. It was then I realised I did not know which of the buildings ahead housed Jock and, not fancying trudging from one to the other, in the heat of the afternoon, decided to ask the askari for directions. At the pace I was walking I was not going to overtake him and as it was too hot to run I stopped, filled my lungs and yelled in my best barrack square voice, "ASKARI!" The figure ahead came to a halt and waited for me to catch up. Upon my sweaty arrival the askari sprang to attention and, with a crisp "Sir!", brought his arm up in a salute. For a moment I was taken aback. He was most informative and directed me to the correct building.

I stayed with Jock for an evening meal and then, together with a friend of his, we set off back to town to indulge in what was, apparently, the expatriate's Saturday night out - the equivalent of a pub crawl, only we went from ship to ship at the docks.

Jock's friend was rather garrulous and became more so as the evening progressed. He informed me, after our arrival at the dockside, that if you wandered slowly past the dockside shipping, glancing through the portholes, there was always the chance there "might be something going on". The story he related, and no doubt it had been told many times before, was of a young couple caught coupling. He described sexual activity so arduous that it must surely have rocked the boat. I suspected this was the only time he had satisfied his frustrated lust and the relating of it gave him a secondary satisfaction. I was rather relieved we saw nothing.

I do not think I could have stomached the undoubted gloating it would have spawned.

We finished the evening at the British Club, where a dance was in progress, and joined friends of Jock's at a table. When the dance finished the band struck up the British National Anthem. Before its conclusion one of the coloured waiters began to talk to his companion. He was soundly cursed by a large, red-faced club member for 'his bloody cheek', thereby causing a greater disturbance than the one of which the latter complained.

Late Sunday morning I accompanied my hangover to the hotel terrace where Jock and friends had gathered, prior to going up the coast for a picnic. The day was heavy and humid and the sun seemed to reflect from everything with unusual intensity; colours assuming the brilliance of back-lit stained glass. An effect my eyes could not dwell upon for any length of time. I was not suffering alone. The others were wearing dark-glasses and expressions of fragility. For the most part they gave wan smiles and gentle nods of the head in greeting each other. I waved them goodbye as they drove off, feeling not a little envious of them for they would soon have the salve of a cool sea to help disperse their hangovers.

The train was due to leave late that afternoon and after a rather meagre lunch I left the hotel and set off to the station. When the train arrived I noticed there was no corridor in that part of the train in which I had been booked. I drew the Indian official's attention to this, for it appeared I had no access to the dining-car.

"You will have to get out, at one stop, and walk along to the dining-car. Then, when the train stops again, you can get out and return to your compartment." With this quick explanation he was away before my befuddled brain had taken in the implications of what he had said. I boarded the train with the thought that at least I had the compartment to myself.

I sank back into a few nostalgic memories as the train passed over the causeway to the mainland and continued through some somewhat uninteresting landscape. Then, for a while, I read a book until the sky darkened with the oncoming of night and I was obliged to switch on the none too bright compartment light. My stomach appeared to have recovered from its earlier queasiness and seemed ready to accept its normal quota of food. I decided to leave the train at the next opportunity and make my way forward to the dining-car. But, when we made our first stop, I discovered that the part of the train which contained my carriage was a long way from the station. Below, some three feet below, lay rough trackside terrain. Hunger overcoming any scruples I had, I dropped down and reached up to close the door, before walking over the uneven ground towards the front of the train.

I had not gone far before the thought of 'How will I recognise my compartment again?' stopped me. Turning, I realised my return might pose problems. I cursed myself for not having enough savvy to have put a piece of paper in the door; or a handkerchief tied to the door handle. But ideas, like apologies, often come too late.

The meal was worth the effort, even though I hurried to finish before the train stopped at another station. At last, walking back into the blackness, broken now and then by the glow from a few compartments, I considered what I would do should the train begin to leave before I was aboard. This pushed me into making an effort to get on the train as quickly as possible. There was a compartment with a light on in the middle of an adjacent carriage. Gently and slowly I eased myself up, like a thief in the night, until I could see into the compartment; hoping I would not be confronted by a Mombasa porthole episode. It was unoccupied and I could have shouted with relief when I saw the book I had been reading lying on the seat. I climbed in and at the same time resolved that if I was obliged to go through this performance again I would buy something for an evening meal earlier in the day. Walking the track at night was definitely out. My hands were filthy with dust and sooty deposit so I undressed, washed and went to bed.

Next morning I gathered my things together early, for we were due in Nairobi that morning. Thank goodness the platform was long enough for the full length of the train. At the station we were greeted by an overcast sky and a generally cold and bleak atmosphere. This change in the climate was totally unexpected after the rather oppressive humidity of the coast. As the train was not due to leave for over an hour I took the opportunity to contact Ross Innes' office. Unfortunately he was not there that morning, so I left a message. On my return to the train I was approached by the Traffic Manager who explained, to my relief, that I had been given the wrong compartment at Mombasa and that my correct accommodation was near the front of the train. Here the coaches had corridors giving access to the dining-car so it appeared that my immediate worries were over.

I shared my new compartment with an Assistant District Commissioner from the Upper Nile Province of the Sudan and a university student, home on holiday from England. The latter was seen off by his mother whose parting remark to him, as the train drew out of the station, was "Have a good trek." I looked at the student with renewed interest. Perhaps my first impression of him as a rather colourless character was totally wrong. But, somehow, the comfortable sports-coat, grey flannel trousers, together with the straw hat set above a pale pimply face, could not be associated with the word 'Trek.' I had always thought it synonymous with vast open spaces; oxen straining, with eyes rolling at the crack of whips and dust-stained people stumble-walking with weariness alongside their wagons under a hot sun. A little romantic, maybe, but my fellow-traveller sitting opposite me, with camera and map, did not look like he was about to undergo any great exertion, or mind-bending experience.

Later, during introductions, the student told us he was going as far as Nimule on the Uganda/Sudan border, but would be breaking his Journey to see Thompson's Falls before returning by the same route.

I derived some satisfaction that my own 'Trek' was further than his, and this went some way to nullify the effect of his snobbish attitudes. As typified by his comment, when I exposed my plebeian origins by stating that I would be taking an early tea.

"Oh," he commented, "we never have dinner before nine at home - often much later."

I thought - you pompous pimply pratt!

The A.D.C. looked across at me and grimaced. He and I had struck up a certain rapport, due to our common destination, and he was more than a match for him. Frequently deflating his ego when he came on a little too strong.

We passed the time talking, playing cards, reading, or just looking out of the window. The others had seen this type of country before but I enjoyed the novelty of the unknown. Now and again the student went to the window and took a photograph and then, carefully consulting his map to pin-point where and what had been taken, he noted it down in a book. He showed neither joy nor enthusiasm for what he was doing and I began to wonder if these two qualities were alien to him.

During our progress into the Kenya Highlands the temperature dropped considerably. I was totally unprepared for the change and shivered in my thin, khaki-drill suit. In my ignorance, I had assumed that the line of the Equator meant heat, but crossing the Equator at 9,000 feet, my muscles were continually tensed against the cold as we breathed vapour against the inside of the compartment windows. But the outside air was wonderfully clear; the undulating landscape hard etched against a sparkling blue sky. For the most part it was like an English Spring and after the heat and humidity of the past two months my body felt alive again. Here, in the hills, the local natives wore heavier clothing. At one stop a group of men wore thick woollen top-coats, long trousers tucked into high fitting 'cowboy boots', check shirts and stetson hats. This attire was the exception, the majority wore the more conventional open-necked shirt and shorts; the women brightly coloured print dresses.

Passing through Eldoret and Namasalgali we came to the Masindi Hotel, where we stayed overnight. Here was the unexpected luxury of a double room. I stretched out comfortably on the bed beneath the cool sheets. There was no stuffy mosquito netting, as in Zanzibar, for doors and windows were wired against them.

After breakfast next morning we travelled by coach to Butiaba, a small town on the edge of Lake Albert. Here the native Customs officers made the most of examining our papers and passports, no doubt glad to exercise their authority. We then boarded the steamer which was to take us to the lake's northern shore and where the Nile began. We had not progressed far when we were obliged to take shelter to avoid a vast cloud of midges, hanging low over the water in our path. On arrival we disembarked and boarded the steamer for the final stage of our journey to the Sudan. In contrast to the propeller-driven steamer we had just left it was paddle-driven and was not unlike a matchbox with a funnel to look at. The paddles were situated at the stern, making it easier for the steamer to reverse should the bows, or side barges, become stuck on a mud bank. The barges fulfilled a dual purpose, not only carrying cargo, but also serving to stabilise the top heavy vessel. The lower deck contained the engine-room, the centre main deck was for passenger use and accommodation, while the upper consisted of the bridge and Captain's quarters. This was the boat which was to take us down the upper reaches of the Nile. As far as we were concerned a relaxing journey, but this vicinity was once popularised by controversial Victorian exploration. Men such as Speke, Burton, Grant, Baker, Livingstone and Stanley experienced trials and frustrations beyond our imagination, beside which our worries over a few items of luggage palled into insignificance.

But, as far as we were concerned, for a few days we could relax and get to know our fellow passengers - should we wish. I met the Boltons - Len and Irene - two South Africans returning to Juba from leave. I was later to become friendly with them, visiting their home when survey work took me to Juba. It was they who warned me against drinking ship-board water as it came straight out of the Nile; recommending instead soft drinks from bottles. Apart from the various bugs in the water it was easy to realise why the seasonal flooding of parts of Egypt was so beneficial to agriculture in that country. Throughout the river's progression millions of animals, fish and fowl must defecate into the Nile during its journey of some 4,000 miles from the heart of Africa to the Mediterranean Sea.

As we progressed slowly downstream our days were spent sunning ourselves on deck and observing, usually at early morning, the species of animals who came to drink, or graze, at the water's edge. In the more distant grassland, elephant and various types of gazelle, buck and antelope turned to gaze as we passed, or suspiciously moved away. Watching them from a distance I found these tantalising glimpses somewhat unsatisfactory and would have relished a closer acquaintanceship. This was compensated to some extent by the aquatic life of the river. Hippo constantly amused us by their antics as their heads bobbed above the surface inquisitively, or maybe resentfully; snorting through large, bulbous nostrils, or flicking water in all directions with pink patterned prominent ears. And, not so conspicuously, the crocodiles; ever-watchful, ever-hopeful, nose-pushing through the water like so many rough-barked, flattened logs, with steady predatory gaze.

The rainy season was not yet over and one day, at the threat of a heavy storm, the steamer was anchored in mid-stream until it had passed. First came the wind, with gradually increasing force, until the canvas deck-screens flapped in a wild dance. Driven before the wind was a wide, grey wall of rain, moving inexorably towards us, swallowing up the landscape as it came. Visibility was cut to one hundred yards, then fifty. The bank on the windward side disappeared from view. The river's surface became agitated like a frenzy of fish at a trout-farm feeding time. Simultaneously the deck was spattered by great drops of rain and we hurriedly took shelter on the other side of the boat until the torrential downpour had swept over. The Captain's tactic in anchoring in mid-stream was normal practice in the circumstances for, should the side-barges run aground, or break free, there was always the chance the steamer would turn turtle.

The morning of our arrival at Nimule, on the Uganda-Sudan border, I awoke to the sound of a rifle shot, followed in quick succession by another. I went out on deck. The Captain was standing upon the bridge, rifle in hand, looking intently towards the near-shore. I looked in the direction of his gaze but saw nothing of interest. Later, at breakfast, he explained that he had been driving away crocodiles who had become interested in the activities of one of the crew members, who was fishing. The latter must have had some success for there was fish on the menu for breakfast. A fellow passenger commented, after tasting his portion, that it had a muddy flavour. The general consensus of opinion was that the fish should have been left to the crocodiles.

Nimule was marked rather grandiosely in large print on the map, so that its rather desolate appearance, in reality, was unexpected. In view was a single, large storage shed, a little distance from the landing-stage. Otherwise, the only indication of human habitation, or presence, was an old native attired in a well-worn ex-army cap, baggy coat and trousers and clutching a battered bugle in his hand. Passengers who had been this way before had warned of his inevitable presence upon the boat's arrival. He suddenly sprang to attention, raised the bugle to his lips, then gave us his version of 'Come to the Cookhouse Door, Boys'. The result, I fear, was not what the maker of the instrument had intended, for it sounded like an asthmatic peacock. We gave him some money to shut him up. Which made us both happy - but for different reasons.

Spacious station-wagons of the Sudan Railways arrived not long after we had unloaded our belongings and, dispersed among them, we waved goodbye to those remaining on the boat and set off northwards along a dusty, loose-surfaced road. Past small roadside villages, where the inhabitants waved as we swept by and young, naked children shouted and danced excitedly. I looked at villages and people with interest for, in all probability, this area could well come within the scope of my forthcoming survey.

It took us some four hours to reach the Nile ferry, which would take us across to Juba, the Equatorial Province capital and administrative centre. As we waited for the steamer to come across I could see that the opposing bank sloped slightly upwards. Just over the ridge I was able to make out a number of scattered huts, with their ubiquitous thatched roofs, together with several grayish white buildings. Was this Juba? No; it was not until we had crossed over and climbed the rising ground that the town proper came into view. First, we passed the grouped huts of the native quarter, with their sickly smelling latrines close-by. The familiar piss-smell I later got to know so well, when I came back from my journeys to the East Bank. Then, the tall tower of the mosque stood out; then the more substantial Government buildings, though few in number, and the more numerous bungalow-type homes of European Government officials, together with those of wealthy Arabs and other trading nationals.

We were deposited in the lounge of the Juba Hotel, where Northern Sudanese officials examined our passports and asked questions before finally stamping in our visas which, in my case, was to last for two years. Jimmy Roscoe, the local BELRA worker at Lui whom, so I had been told would meet me, was not there when I arrived. However, a grey-haired, sparse-looking man in his sixties approached me and introduced himself as the local Archdeacon of the Church Missionary Society. He explained that Jimmy Roscoe had been detained, until the following day, and it had been arranged for me to stay overnight at his house. Upon arrival I was introduced to his wife who, if anything, was leaner than he and equally grey-haired. That evening, over a meal, we made polite conversation during which they told me they had worked in the Sudan since before the war. Afterwards we listened to the BBC Overseas Service on their radio. But briefly, as the car battery was used by the simple expedient of running a wire out through the window to the wagon parked up close outside.

The next morning I had occasion to use the outhouse. It contained a red flag attached to a pole and which, so I was told later, was usually pushed through a gap in the wall to indicate to potential users that the place was occupied. In a busy household I could see the advantage of this relict of Victorian prudery and wondered if one waved the flag about if you ran out of toilet paper. When not in use the flag was tucked away out of sight. Early next day I was introduced to an Irish couple, the husband being the organisation's local accountant and through whom I would be paid, then Lucy at the Sudan Bookshop, which was run by the CMS[*].

Jimmy Roscoe arrived late in the afternoon. A rather stocky, tubby figure, dressed in shorts and safari-jacket who, after the formal introductions, explained that as it would entail a long trip

---

[*] Church Missionary Society

back to Lui in the dark, he thought it advisable to stay overnight at the Mission Station at Lanya where he, his wife and son, had spent the previous night. I was introduced to Manoa, the Lui colony driver, a slightly built Moru who limped from a partially disabled leg, but who generally looked upon the world with a big grin.

It was dark well before we had gone halfway on our sixty mile journey, so that I saw little of the countryside. Suddenly, as we were crossing a small bridge over a culvert, some five miles from Lanya, a tyre burst and the pick-up slewed across the road into a drainage ditch. I hung onto the door of the vehicle, anticipating it might turn over. But we were lucky for the pick-up lurched to a halt in the soft bed of the ditch, sinking into the loose earth and making it necessary to raise the axle in order to change the wheel. But the jack proved useless, as it sank into the soft ground; stones were needed to give it a solid base. Jimmy handed me a torch and suggested I find some. Fear of the unknown is one of man's greatest fears, especially if tempered by the related experiences of others, as had mine. The previous evening I had been regaled with stories of lion, leopard, buffalo and hunting dogs, at the Archdeacon's and, if all was to be believed, I didn't stand a prayer. I was, therefore, less than enthusiastic with my designated task.

Just out of range of the pick-up's headlights I was aware of the insignificant glow afforded by the torch. I felt as if I were trying to illuminate the world's largest cave with a candle. Surely the lights would attract animals to the spot - like moths to a candle? Lions to a torch? I glanced furtively around, expecting at any moment to see the green reflecting glow from a lion's eyes, or hear the angry snort of a buffalo. I began whistling softly to myself - to 'keep my pecker up' - as I had done when a boy, passing a churchyard at night. I walked further up the road in my search for large stones. From the surrounding grasses came the 'Tink-tink-tink' of Bell-frogs. They seemed happy enough. I scuffed the ground at my feet, to emphasise my 'search', then returned to the others to pronounce my efforts unsuccessful. Manoa rather spoilt it by arriving at the same moment with a pile of stones. Eventually, with a shovel borrowed from a nearby roadworker's hut, we dug ourselves out, changed the wheel and arrived at Lanya two hours later than expected.

The next morning, accompanied now by Jimmy's wife and young son John, we set off for Lui. After the well-surfaced roads of Zanzibar the road to Lui was but a track. Later, I was surprised to find out that it was the best road in the Province and one of the few open to traffic throughout the year. Lui, at first sight, was pleasing enough; the greens of the grasses, shrubs and trees contrasting with grey-black irregular-shaped, rocky outcrops on the surrounding hummocky hills. I thought I would enjoy my stay.

Chapter 9

I awoke next morning in my temporary home. The bedroom - and only habitable room - contained the basic essentials of a bed (be-decked with the ubiquitous mosquito-net), a small table, under one of the two fly-wired windows, and a chair upon which to place my torch at night.

The white-washed walls, while austerely bare, created an aura of coolness during the heat of the day. A door led out to a small, low-walled veranda at the rear and the area proved to be a welcome retreat, for it was in shadow most of the time. Another door opened onto the long open-sided veranda which ran the length of the front part of the house; leading, at the far end, into what once had been the living/dining room. The floors were of a hard, red-coloured composition, with a polished surface. Entering this room, now bereft of doors and windows, I intruded upon the drowsy moments of numerous lizards enjoying the early sun. They panicked and, in their haste to make an escape, skidded across the floor with uncontrolled movements, like disorientated ice-dancers. I smiled at their antics but retreated so as not to frighten them farther.

There was a small bathroom at the opposite end of the veranda, adjacent to the bedroom. The bath, made from cement, tended to be a little on the abrasive side. This, and its short length, did not encourage prolonged immersion. A small bracket in the corner was for a lamp, it usually being after dusk before you bathed. The used water ran away through a pipe into a bucket or other receptacle outside, to be re-cycled in the garden. At the side of this drain stood a raised oil-drum, lying long ways and which, when filled, was heated by a fire underneath to provide hot water for the bath.

A few yards away a species of Magnolia tree's cool-white flowers and foliage half-hid the outhouse. I found the interior dim and dank after the heat and brightness of the morning sun when I first sought to use it. Lifting the hinged seat I was somewhat taken aback to hear a buzz of excitement - or was it expectancy? - from the depths. The sound increased. I hurriedly sat down to find, to my consternation, my bottom being buffeted by flies. Of a fair size too judging by the impact. Not that I blamed them for wanting to escape from their putrescent pit but, knowing where they'd been and my imagination taking over, I retired as quickly as possible, feeling somewhat unclean.

I had received my initiation into Lui latrines the previous evening after a meal at the Roscoes'. What began as a guide to local wild life, allied with people's experiences with lions, leopards and buffalo whilst on trek, eventually centred on the smaller, more mundane species of life. They told, not without humour, of the time Jim West, one of the CMS doctors at Lui Hospital, had found, after dropping his shorts in the loo, that he had the company of a snake. Without bothering to pull up his shorts he short-stepped his way to safety. Having been made aware of the danger of scorpions by Ross Innes I had already schooled myself to tap out my shoes before putting them on. But now I was informed that scorpions were also prone to high-tailing it down from thatched roofs of out-buildings - as were spiders, snakes and lesser known species of African life.

I smiled at their stories, where I thought I should smile, but no doubt my eyes betrayed the apprehension I felt at times. I was affected in another more natural way when my bowels began to churn and eventually I could not delay my need to use the toilet any longer. I was directed towards a dark shape at the end of a dirt path, with a final "Watch out for scorpions." and a flickering torch. The door was ill-fitting and I had to apply pressure to open it as it scraped over the tightly packed earth of the floor. Shining the torch quickly around the thatched roof, I then placed it on the seat. For one fearful moment I considered going back to the house, but nature was not to be denied. Quickly, I had

> The seat up
>
> Trousers down
>
> Sat down
>
> Bore down
>
> Stood up
>
> Wiped up
>
> Trousers up
>
> Seat down
>
> And out!

"All right?" enquired my hosts, raising an eyebrow in surprise at my rapid return.

"All right." I confirmed. At the same time making a mental note to regulate my lavatorial visits to the day-time, if possible.

A previous occupier of the premises, a clergyman of the CMS I believe, had left evidence of his hunting prowess in the form of seven or eight sun-bleached buffalo skulls, complete with horns. They hung somewhat precariously, if the tilt of one or two of them was anything to go by, along the front veranda where they gleamed into a life of atrophied trophy at the coming of a new day.

I pondered upon reincarnation and wondered if the hunter returned in some shape or form to become the hunted; or to be haunted, by his victims. My thoughts, straying dangerously near the periphery of philosophy, were brought down to earth by the sudden appearance upon the road ahead of me of a nubile young school-girl of some fourteen or fifteen years. As she walked, her brown buttocks jiggled either side of a small bunch of leaves which, together with a similar bunch at the front, was all she wore. Both bunches held in place by a thin cord secured around her loins. Such an unaccustomed sight (at that time) giving rise to day-dreams which, no doubt, I thought, would later transmogrify into the reality, and at times embarrassing inconvenience, of wet-dreams. Hardly the thoughts to take with me to breakfast at the Roscoes'. But then, they weren't to know!

The BELRA supervisor's house occupied by Jimmy and family lay about a quarter of a mile from the colony centre and adjacent to the main road to Juba. The well-established garden complimented the red-brick walls and grass-thatched roof which, extending outwards, sheltered the open-sided veranda that ran almost completely around the sides of the dwelling. Brick supporting pillars rose up from the concrete-floored veranda and, near the front entrance, several old petrol tins held Marjorie Roscoe's pride and joy - six flourishing geraniums. Jimmy had attempted to express his horticultural aspirations with several tin-planted strawberry plants. But, as he was quick to point out at my somewhat questioning gaze, they were grown as more of a challenge against the environment than for the table. What strawberries ripened were promptly gulped down by the boys' marauding chickens. Birds late for the feast had vented their disappointment by decimating the leaves.

A semi-circular drive-way came in at the far left-hand corner of the front garden, re-entering the main road in line with the front door of the house. A large fig tree was the prominent feature of the part of the garden bordered by the drive and the tall roadside hedge. Beneath the tree the ground was covered with clumps of wild iris, while a little to one side a single wax-white flowered and sweet-smelling frangi-pangi tree spread its crooked growth.

The Roscoe poultry were in a small pen at the rear of the house - a Rhode Island Red cockerel and five hens. They appeared huge in comparison with the local fowls.

"We have to watch them," commented Jimmy, "especially the eggs. The local natives will give their eye-teeth for fertilised eggs to hatch out and improve their own stock. That's one thing you'll have to watch out for when you take over."

After breakfast on our first morning Jimmy took me down to the colony to introduce me to the patients and staff and familiarise me with the general layout and routine. We walked the back track from the house, passing cultivated plots belonging to the house-boys, then on to the colony itself.

In the early days of their establishment the hospital, leprosy colony and schools at Lui had all come under the jurisdiction of the Church Missionary Society. Initially the colony comprised of some fourteen small huts and a treatment room. Entry to the colony was on a voluntary basis and the afflicted among the local Moru tribe were reluctant to enter. However, a small group of patients were forced to enter by the local District Commissioner with, no doubt, strong enough threats to keep them there. Tribesmen from outside the district drifted in hoping for a quick cure, to leave when they realised little or nothing could be done for them.

By about 1928 there were fifty patients at Lui and, although many were far from satisfied with their lot, because of their enforced detainment, there was some consolation in a roof over their heads and food rations. At the turn of the decade conditions improved when additional buildings were made available.

Somewhat strict rules were enforced by the missionary-in-charge. Patients were forbidden to marry, or have children, and the punishment for breaching these regulations was ten lashes of the whip. While deemed necessary from the European point of view, such restrictions were completely alien to the natural inclinations and traditions of the natives. No doubt the medical reasons for the rules were never adequately explained. However, the patients won out in the end and were eventually allowed to marry. But, as a compromise, children of the union were taken away from the mother after the weaning stage and cared for by a woman living outside the colony, who was paid five shillings a month for her trouble. The procedure thus established was far ahead of the treatment itself. In later years, in other leprosaria, the practice of separating mother and child became standard. Mothers were allowed to wean their children while dressed in protective clothing, so as to prevent general skin-to-skin contact. After weaning, mothers were allowed to see their children only from a distance.

In 1940 a BELRA supervisor was appointed to Lui and the colony became a separate unit from the Mission hospital. This had been found to be necessary as the running of the colony had developed into a full-time job and had become an administrative burden to the hospital staff.

As we entered the outskirts of the colony Jimmy pointed out a large plot of cultivated ground on our left. "Ground-nuts," he said. "The older boys look after them and the harvest is shared among them and those in the colony unable to fend for themselves."

We passed by the huts, school and church, to finally arrive at a small brick-built complex consisting of the treatment centre and stores. While I was being introduced to the colony staff the patients inspected me from a distance. I was surprised by the absence of advanced cases among the patients and commented upon the fact.

"Our policy is," Jimmy explained, "that treatment of children should be given priority. Generally speaking, there is more chance of affecting a cure if you catch the disease early. Here, we tend to specialise in the treatment of children. You will see a few old cases here, still receiving some form of treatment, but most are burnt-out, usually leaving behind some crippling deformity of the hands, feet or both." I nodded in acknowledgement. My companion was reiterating much of what Ross Innes had told me earlier.

"You see," he continued, "these children invariably contract leprosy from parents or relatives who, in their turn, quite possibly were infected by their parents, or some close relation. It's a close contact social disease - aided by the living conditions and habits of the people. The only way to break the cycle is by removing the children from their homes before the disease has progressed too far. We can then more or less guarantee a high percentage of cures."

"But surely," I pointed out, "the risk of infection when they return home must be high?" Jimmy shrugged his shoulders. "We can just hope the rudimentary rules of hygiene we teach them will help."

All my work to date had been concerned with the statistical and survey side of the problem. I had only vague ideas as to the methods of treatment employed; my practical medical training was virtually non-existent, unlike Jimmy Roscoe who had come to the work with some nursing experience behind him. I thus awaited the first treatment day with interest. Drugs were given both orally and by injection. The children were, almost without exception, given injections of Sulphetrone, the dosage varying with the age of the child. While many grimaced with pain as they were injected, the treatment was a great advance on that of injecting hydnocarpus oil. The latter was injected inter-dermally around a lesion, to form a barrier against its spread. While there had been a certain limited amount of success with this over the years, it did not guarantee a cure. The injections were painful to the patient due to the density of the oil, which did not disperse but gave rise to swelling under the skin. The procedure was tedious and tiring to the person administering the treatment, for quite an amount of force was required to expel the oil from the hypodermic syringe. Some of the patients at Lui were still given oil injections, but these were advanced cases who would not have benefited from modern drugs as their disease had all but run its natural course, as they entered the burnt-out stage.

Adult patients were given tablets of Diamino-diphenyl-sulphone (DDS), as were a few children in whom the disease was well advanced.

"You have to be careful with DDS," cautioned Jimmy, "it should only be given under strict supervision, with a constant check made on the patient's reaction to the drug. Some patients can cope with a higher dosage than others. Those unable to tolerate what is considered to be a normal dose experience a violent reaction and become quite ill. We've a young girl here at the moment who has developed a severe lepra reaction to DDS."

He led the way out from the dispensary to one of the women's huts. Several elderly women were seated inside. A young girl was lying on a rough wooden bed. The old women greeted us as we entered. The girl was a lepromatus type and her physical condition had been exaggerated by the drug, causing parts of her face and body to swell up grotesquely.

"She's much better now," said Jimmy, "and most of the fever she had has gone. But I think you'll appreciate how careful you have to be with the treatments. At the first sign of a reaction you must stop the treatment immediately and on no account continue until the reaction is over. A record must be kept of the dosage so that you will know, in such cases, when saturation point has been reached. Then, in future, your treatment must be below that level. The essential thing to remember is that the drug is highly toxic and must not be administered haphazardly. In the outstations it's not possible to supervise the treatments, as you only visit once a month and treatments, of course, are carried out weekly. You have to rely on the dressers-in-charge."

I wondered how I would fare on my own, when I had to take over from the Roscoes. Jimmy must have read my thoughts and continued. "You're lucky here. Most of the staff are quite reliable and the head-dresser was a medical assistant at Juba Civil Hospital, until he was sent here for treatment. So the actual treatment side of things should give you little trouble. Anyhow, if you need help, have a word with the medical staff at the hospital."

For which information I offered up a silent prayer.

Chapter 10

Extending from the church to the eastern side of the small colony plots was an open stretch of green, used by the schoolchildren as a playing field and for special occasions. Around the perimeter of the green were placed the huts for women and girls, while those for the boys and men were situated at the western end of the ground.

The cultivation areas, where crops were grown for the general use of the colony, bordered the living quarters and, apart from these sections of general husbandry, patients who were capable of gardening for themselves were allocated plots for their own use. There was also an acre or so of land given over to the growing of cotton. A new venture by Jimmy Roscoe, in the hope that the colony would ultimately make its own bandages. But the project had not taken off, as hoped, because no one knew how to work the small hand-loom which had been made available. A section of swampy ground had been sown with rice and this experiment had met with some success, the crop supplementing the patients' everyday diet of cassava or grain.

Water for the community came from a deep well with a less regular supply from a stream which flowed along one side of the colony perimeter. Towards the end of the rainy season this stream was dammed to ensure a subsidiary supply of water during the dry season. At times it was difficult to gauge when the rains had ended and, on several occasions, late rains had damaged or washed away the dams.

Lui was one of few stations to have water on tap. Pumped from the stream into a large metal tank on the brow of a rocky, ironstone outcrop, the water was then piped down to the Roscoes' house and to the nearby Church Missionary Hospital. The flow was carefully controlled by a stop-cock in the Roscoes' garden and the water turned on for a short period only, to allow for the basic needs of the day. Towards the end of the dry season, when the water level in the tank had dropped to but a foot or so, the water's surface tended to become covered with green growth which appeared to add a slightly offensive quality to the bath water. Concerned with what hidden health hazard might be brewing within, I heavily dosed it with Dettol. A practice I maintained whether in the house or out on trek.

Lining the road between the Roscoes' and the CMS hospital were large, towering Kapok trees; a source of pillow stuffing for both Europeans and local natives. The latter flaying the trees with long bamboo poles to dislodge the mature seed pods, which were up to some five inches long, with a thin, hard fibrous coating. Spheroid in shape and tapering to a point at each end, the pods contained a compact mass of white, silky fibres which, in turn, enfolded numerous black seeds. The separation of seeds from fibres was commonly achieved by putting the contents of the pods in a four-gallon petrol tin and shaking vigorously up and down, causing the seeds to filter through to the bottom of the can. Many of the Kapok trees in this area of the Southern Sudan were said to have been originally planted by Northern Arab slavers to mark their route and resting places. Older local inhabitants had bitter memories of how ancestors had been taken during this period. Arab caravans traded in and around Azande country which lay on the west of the southern Sudan and adjacent to the Belgian Congo.

Their basic items of trade were ivory and slaves, from about 1860. By 1870 the Egyptian government sent its forces to the area, which confused the issue. The situation was further aggravated by an influx of conquering Dervishes who, in turn, caused confusion and chaos by their cruelty.

At early evening, prior to going to the Roscoes' for my evening meal, I soaked in a basically-built cement bath. One of the hazards when making use of this facility was that its rough surface tended to cause a slight degree of flagellation to the buttocks. Unless you sat with a minimum of movement.

Sometimes, whilst in the bath, I had visitors; inquisitive, low-flying bats who caused me to duck and weave quite unnecessarily. It was possible to adapt to their lantern induced shadows on the wall but, on one occasion, I was startled by a bat which came too close for comfort and, hitting out, knocked it to the floor. I watched as it crawled slowly and laboriously to a wall. Here it struggled upwards until, having gained sufficient height it swooped downwards, then upwards, to disappear from view in the dark shadowed recesses of the roof. In time, I became used to the creatures' nocturnal visits. After all, it was their home before I arrived. Another intruder of sorts was a frog which shared the bath, living in the exit drain. During the day its raucous unmusical voice could be heard at intervals emanating from its home. Quite possibly protesting at its nightly immersion in soapy suds.

Occasionally, when I left the house to go to the Roscoes' for my evening meal, I turned to face the house frontage and shone my torch upon the large-headed, skeletal, buffalo skulls. Moving the light from side to side had the effect of causing elongated shadows which, in turn, generated a macabre impression of life after death, a fragment of make believe which I did not pursue having, on a dark night, to walk a lonely road. Besides, there was a natural nightly phenomenon - the march of the black ants. Down the road they came in a long line undisturbed by the light of the torch. They were returning to their nest, which lay at the roadside and close to the end of the path leading to the house. A closer inspection showed that the centre of the column consisted of ants carrying items necessary for the benefit of the colony. The two sides of the line were patrolled by a larger type of ant whose job was obviously to protect the workers and what they carried. That there was a need for this was proved all too clearly when, near the entrance to the nest, red robber ants lay in ambush, and it was in this area that bitter fighting took place.

Ants abounded everywhere. Black, red, white - large and small. There was always one species or another to be seen. The root area of the hedge near the Roscoes' house was the favoured living area of the 'Spider' ants. These were rather large and, as the name implies, were similar in appearance to spiders. They were to be seen industriously occupied in underground improvements to their nest, bringing stones and debris to the surface. This was then deposited in a growing heap encircling the entrance to the nest. A species of red ant frequented the region of the water-control point in the Roscoes' garden. Their son John's curiosity resulted in his being frequently bitten. Small Argentinian ants were habitual incomers to houses, where they cleared up crumbs of food and carried off dead insects who had met their death by spraying, or incineration by oil lamps. Sometimes, the insect's size necessitated group cooperation, although, now and again, some pushed and some pulled in opposite directions so that the insect remained where it was. The hardened earth structures of white ants were ubiquitous and of variable design. Some were tall, tapering pillars; others similar in appearance to mushrooms, about nine inches across at the top. On some of the more isolated roads their handiwork protruded up as far as the under-side of vehicles, anything over this being removed. Perhaps their greatest inconvenience was intrusion into the thatched roof of a house.

Another type of black ant, of a roving nature and ferocious demeanour constructed a half-round tunnel, commonly seen going across the dirt roads. We had run over these on many occasions and one day, this having occurred again, I told Manoa, the colony driver, to stop the pickup while I walked back to satisfy my curiosity. When I was within two yards of the scene my curiosity was more than satisfied when dozens of ants poured out of the gaps made by the tyres and came directly towards me. At this juncture I decided that discretion was called for and beat an undignified retreat. Manoa told me (better late than never) that insects, small rodents and even snakes had been overwhelmed and become part of the ants' food-chain.

My interest in ants was not without its repercussions. One evening I was awakened by something crawling across my chest, followed by several unknown entities racing down the side of my body. In a state of mild panic I fumbled to pull out the mosquito net in order to grab my torch from the small bedside chair. Quickly I shone its beam on my body, where the invaders were still jostling around. And there, in the light of the torch, I saw the ants. Or rather, what I thought to have been ants, were but mobile beads of perspiration.

Ross Innes had warned me of one potential danger - the scorpion. To simplify its description one could compare it with the common earwig, only more lethal. One danger was that the scorpion had a liking for footwear left by the side of your bed overnight. So the practice of tapping out your shoes each morning became part of the daily routine. I did not encounter the scorpion under these circumstances, but was once offered one at a market. The man showed it to me resting on the palm of his hand. He offered to transfer it over to my hand. But I noticed that his hand was covered with thick leathery skin and so the front pincers could not obtain a grip needed for leverage to bring over the long tail with its poisoned sting. The skin on my own hands was comparatively soft and would have left me 'ripe for the kill', had I taken up the challenge.

Saturday night was the highlight of the week for, upon this day, supplies and mail arrived from Juba, visiting various stations on route. It then carried on to Zambia, Meredi and - if I remember rightly - to Yei. It then returned on the same route, this time taking orders and mail to Juba. The hard used vehicle carried outside-passengers, balancing precariously and clinging to handholds for dear life and with a prayer, if of Christian persuasion and otherwise, if Pagan.

I was walking down the road with Jimmy when he suddenly put a hand on my arm, at the same time saying urgently, "Stop! You're standing on a snake!" I stood still. Then I looked down at my feet where one of my size 9 shoes was firmly planted just behind the head of the squirming snake. Its discomfort was only too obvious, emphasised by agitated flicking of its tongue in and out of its mouth which was, fortunately for me, facing away from my foot. I tensed myself before leaving my position by accomplishing the longest standing-jump I had ever made, or expect to do again. I hit the ground running, joined by Jimmy, both of the unspoken opinion that any delay might have drawn retaliation from an obviously bloody-minded snake.

While I had been given a broad knowledge of the working of Lui Leprosarium, for when I took over from Jimmy when he went on leave, I responded most to the monthly visits to the outstations. These treatment centres came under the jurisdiction of the Superintendent at Lui who was responsible for supplying medical and food requirements. The chiefs of each area, where the centre was located, were responsible for repairs to the buildings. Accommodation was limited and it was usually given to advanced cases, such as those who had lost fingers or toes, the disfigurement restricting normal activities. Here they were provided with shelter so had no worries on that score. As at Lui, plots of land were available for crops to supplement the monthly delivery of grain or cassava. During the monthly visit the Lui Superintendent listened to complaints, some of which could be dealt with on the spot. Needs of a medical nature were discussed with the dresser, who sometimes had a history of leprosy himself. The cost of repairs, food and other basic necessities were the responsibility of the Sudan Government. Lui Leprosarium was a separate organisation altogether and its costs were met by BELRA. The outstations were scattered over a wide area and the furthest from Lui was 80 miles away at Meredi.

I had been told, upon my arrival in the Sudan, that my survey work would be among the Bari tribe. It was recommended that I study the language with the help of Andrea Sulle, a Bari, and who was to become my indispensable assistant and interpreter. There was also an added advantage for Andrea had once been successfully treated for leprosy. But when I discovered that most of my survey work would be away from the Bari and with other tribes, I rather ignored this chore and instead discussed with Andrea the various aspects of life generally, instead of pursuing the intricacies of Bari grammar. No doubt, also a linguistic laziness on my part.

In the meantime casual interests took my fancy, even though it was just to linger and admire the multi-coloured butterflies and, in so doing, acquire a sense of joy and tranquillity. I mentioned my interest to Jimmy one day and he confessed that he collected butterflies. I briefly considered following his example but changed my mind when I saw him kill a butterfly by crushing its thorax between his thumb and forefinger. Somewhat sickened by this I reverted to my previous style of interest, convinced that to kill one of a rare species and reduce their number was somehow illogical. There is no equality between a specimen pinned to a card, than on the wing in living flight.

Lizards were always a welcome diversion at times, especially when they provided something unusual; something new. One species frequented the rear of the house on the small veranda, to lie and soak up the morning sun. Easing himself into a satisfactory position a male lizard, whom I had been observing, suddenly thrust his legs up an over his body and onto his back. It was as if he were indulging in some form of reptilian yoga. He lay for a while in a comatose state apparently oblivious to what went on around him. Then, suddenly alerted, he opened his eyes and stared intently down the path. I followed the direction of his gaze to see that the object of his interest was a female of the species. She walked slowly in the sun, oblivious to his looks of adoration.

But her ignorance was soon to be replaced by a rude awareness when, after untangling his legs the male raced down the path towards her. She backed away sharply, then hurriedly made off. But her suitor was quick to follow and, when he caught her up, I saw an amazing sight. The lizard's courtship dance. Stepping up close and facing her he began swaying his head from side to side and with such increasing fervour it almost became a blur. When she turned away he followed her around without losing the tempo of the rather frenzied gyrations of his dance. But the female, possibly having seen it all before, was not over-impressed with his efforts. Obviously a built-in instinct reminding her what lay behind the performance. And so, before the male could finish his routine, she scurried past him and down the path. Catching him on the wrong foot, or dancing step, as it were. I felt for him. All those efforts in vain. He lay, breathing heavily, as he watched her retreat.

Then, with a sudden lease of life he roused himself, for another male lizard had accosted the female, by making an opportunist leap at her from where he had lain hidden in the grass. With a glint of battle in his eyes, our dancing friend summoned up sufficient energy to dive upon the newcomer and at once they were embroiled in battle, with no holds barred, although the favourite grip was upon each other's jaws, as they twisted and turned, seeking advantage. Should a hold be relaxed then one or the other would be thrown violently across the dusty arena. They faced up to each other time and time again, each panting heavily from their exertions. The female had stood off, watching the scene with what appeared to be a considered interest. The newcomer at last conceded the fight and limped away. The victor, with all inclination to dance knocked out of him eased himself, not without some discomfort, to where the object of his desire squatted.

At that moment I felt the need to ease a crick in my neck and moved my head. The slight movement was enough to frighten them both away. I felt somewhat saddened by this, considering that I had broken up what might have proved to be a satisfactory relationship. But then, reasoned that the male, what with his dancing followed by the bout of fighting, may not have had the strength to fulfil his original intention.

Chapter 11

At Juba, during the discussion with the District Commissioner, Reggie Dingwall, and the Province Medical Inspector, Francis Wheaton, it was clear to me that the former would be more deeply involved with the survey than his Medical Service colleague. I suppose this should have been expected as the D.C. had a closer involvement with the local people than did Dr Wheaton. It was the former's helpful suggestions, based upon a deep knowledge of the area, which simplified my work in the initial stages. This being the first survey I had attempted on my own, it was natural I should feel a little apprehensive as to the task ahead.

But a lesser aspect had to be resolved - that of 'Boys'. The wages I was prepared to pay, or rather, could afford to pay, did not bring candidates running from all directions. Those employed by government officials would have openly scoffed at my offer of £2.50 a month for a cook and £2.00 for a house boy.

I was first introduced to Dawedi by one of the CMS workers in Juba. The Irish couple who recommended him for general duties did not suggest he be employed as a cook. A position he would have preferred, both for more money and a higher status. Time was getting short and the need for a cook was somewhat desperate. Then, the day before we were due to leave, the houseboy of a friend brought along an applicant, whom he introduced as his 'brother', and whose reference stated that he had performed some culinary duties to the satisfaction of the writer. With a sense of relief I engaged Dogu on the spot. At least the reference was in his favour, so I decided to take a chance.

Not like the boy who had toured around Juba seeking work

and, no doubt, wondering why the following reference had proved of little use.

"Introducing Wani Modi - my cook for the past two weeks. I found him extremely capable - of anything."

The centre of our first working area was the large village of Liria, about eighty miles from Juba, on the eastern side of the Nile. It was also the home village of Lolik Lado, who was waiting for us at the ferry stage. I greeted him and he replied in his sing-song voice which belied his aura of authority. He wore shirt, slacks and trilby hat and, when not in town, always carried with him his .500 bore rifle, with a belt of cartridges slung across his chest. While we waited for the ferry-boat, the Atbara, to return from the other side, I stood in the shade of a banana tree. Or rather, what I thought was a banana tree until I discovered that, to be botanically correct, it should be referred to as 'a giant perennial herb, resembling a tree'. So, we may add to the old saying "Money doesn't grow on trees" the fact that bananas do not either.

I took in the scene before me. The dozen or so boys splashing at the river's edge, certainly looking less concerned than I felt as I considered what danger they might be in from Crocodile and Hippo. A mother was washing a protesting infant, while other natives drank their fill or washed the dust of travel from their bodies. Most would be returning to their villages, possibly a distance of twenty miles or more. Some were not adverse to asking for a lift. A request from a single man being granted, he would give a shout and a wife, children and a pile of luggage would materialise. There was obviously no room for these extras and when your offer was withdrawn, it gave rise for complaint. Not always based on the refusal, but rather from the fact that the ploy had failed.

The ferry-boat was rather flat, except for the bridge structure situated at the stern of the boat and occupying about a third of the deck space. The sides of the boat were hinged and served as a bridge from boat to shore. The captain and the majority of the crew were Northern Sudanese. After crossing, we travelled south down the Nimule road for some 10 miles, then branched off to the left and eastwards along the Torit road. Thick bush crowded up to the road on both sides, like spectators on a processional route, then, as we neared Liria, the country became more open. There were stretches of grassland lumped with rounded hills, or jebels, to give them the Arabic name commonly used in the Sudan. Young boys were tending sheep and goats in the sun-dried, yellowing pasture. They, the boys, looked up from their charges and tried to prevent them from making potentially suicidal dashes across the road. Then they, goats or sheep, would disappear in the cloud of dust thrown up by the passage of the lorry. When, unexpectedly, any animal raced across your path, it created a double hazard, for itself and the occupants of the vehicle, for to stray off the road meant a possible encounter with stones and rough ground.

We stopped at several villages to allow Lolik Lado to warn the people that they would be surveyed shortly. We left the chief at his Lirian home, one of several homes he had scattered around and in these he had wives at his disposal, so that he could enjoy home comforts and nuptial bliss. Most local chiefs had more than one wife and one old rake of the Moru tribe was said to have, or had, twenty.

Our transport, a hospital lorry, swayed up the rough track which wound its way around the contours of the squat hill overlooking Liria village. The resthouse, situated on the brow, stood out on the sun-scorched rock and sparsely grassed ground, like a hat on a nudist. When our gear had been unloaded I told the driver to return to Juba (as agreed with the hospital) and then return in three days to move us on. This was only an estimate. I had yet to encounter the various aspects of survey work which would have extended the number of days. Originally, I was supposed to have had a lorry and driver of my own for the survey but, in practice, these did not materialise. However, there was some little compensation in the fact that bicycles had been supplied to Andrea and myself for short journeys when on location.

I watched the lorry's progress down the hill and onto the Torit road until it was lost to view behind a small hill. Then I turned and viewed the wide extent of grassland, bearing sporadically low shrub and trees, extending eastwards towards the shoe-shaped hills of the Lameiga area. To the west, isolated and prominent among surrounding cultivation, stood a small collection of brick buildings. These had not been visible from the lower lying road and when I asked Andrea what they might be, he said it was a Catholic Mission. When he added there was also a school there, I made a mental note to visit the latter at the first opportunity.

Until darkness fell there was a continuous procession of villagers to the resthouse, eager to view the newcomers and confirm what our business might be. Or maybe to pick up some town gossip from Juba. At first, I found their continual presence over the following days rather disconcerting, as they watched your every move while you were reading, eating or writing. Leaving you open to identifying habits and idiosyncrasies which gave the native an opportunity to place a nickname, not always a complimentary one, upon you. In turn I glanced over at them now and again, wondering what they were thinking, or why they had laughed. It was hard not to become self-conscious under these circumstances and it took a while to get used to this lack of privacy.

Darkness came with tropical suddenness, the landscape's detail lost as the sun made a swift descent behind the hills. Scores of flickering fires were then clearly visible, patterning the dark shadows of the hillside slopes where the village of Liria lay, like a convention of fireflies. From across the valley came an evening symphony of sounds, as the tinkle of goats' bells and the long drawn-out notes of the horns echoed and mingled with the shouts, screams and singing of the villagers. And, more softly in the immediate vicinity, the throaty croak of bull-frogs and the shrill whining of mosquitoes. The latter intent upon making me part of their evening meal, I retired to bed early, under the protection of a mosquito net.

I was sleeping within the humid confines of the resthouse bedroom. Restless with the heat, I pondered upon the forthcoming work to be done. How would it go? What would be the reaction of the villagers? There was no one to turn to now for advice - I had to make my own decisions. This was an important survey, intensive and the first to have been carried out in the area. I was a little anxious that I might bungle it in some way. In the end I decided that I would have to rely on the gratuitous help of Lolik Lado.

After a rather disappointing breakfast of corned-beef and

scrambled eggs, which somehow Dogu had managed to turn into a culinary disaster, completely unrecognisable and, because I did not fancy the inedible concoction, Andrea and I left at seven o'clock for the village, on our bicycles. On an open space, around an old mango tree, a large crowd had already gathered for our inspection. We greeted the chief and he then proceeded to explain to the villagers the purpose of our visit. They listened attentively to his words, spoken in that sing-song voice of his. Apart from a loincloth the women wore leather aprons, fore and aft, or wore that cheap alternative of bunches of leaves for anatomical privacy. Occasionally, in addition to these sparse coverings the women wore a cloth draped over the body. Children were carried on the hip, while babies occupied goat-skin slings hanging from the mother's shoulder. It was not uncommon to see a young girl of seven or eight years of age carrying around a younger sister, or brother, on her back or hip.

I had intended to use the same methods of examination as those used by Ross Innes, but local circumstances were not favourable to employ them. Several factors contributed to the need to adopt a new system. Firstly, the skin of the Southern Sudanese was black or near black. Ross Innes had warned me that this might prove to be a problem when, in Zanzibar, we had dealt with much lighter-skinned Arab types. Another determinant was that almost without exception, more so among the men and children, their skins had been smeared with dust, making it virtually impossible to discern possible signs of leprosy. Here, Andrea proved his worth. Having had leprosy himself he was competent at diagnosing symptoms, having the ability also to distinguish between the lesions of the disease and old scars which would most certainly have confused me. Although, even he at times would be obliged to ask a suspected case to wash themselves to allow a closer, cleaner inspection. This was particularly so in the case of children.

Without Andrea's assistance in these early stages of the survey, progress would have been extremely slow and frustrating, for I found examining people a slow and laborious job until I became more experienced. Eventually, to save time and unnecessary delay, I let Andrea examine the villagers. Any suspected case he found was asked to stand to one side and then he and I examined that person together. I then classified the type of leprosy and noted relevant details of sex, age etc as we had done on the Zanzibar survey. Infrequently I had to carry on alone when Andrea was sick. This system worked quite well and we used it throughout the survey. Of course, unless there are means of testing suspect cases in a laboratory, it is sometime difficult to be absolutely sure whether or not it is leprosy, or some similar-looking disease. A final opinion of a local person, such as a chief or a native medical dresser would then be advisable. This piece of advice was given to me by Dr Cochrane, BELRA's Medical Secretary just before I left England and, once or twice when Andrea was not available, I was glad to make use of it.

Because of the large numbers of people presenting themselves we worked all through the morning and then, after a brief break for lunch, worked until early evening. At the end of the day, when we were relaxing, a few stragglers came to the resthouse, bringing the flies with them. Dawedi, with a distinct lack of social sensitivity, stimulated by a sense of hygiene, sprayed the newcomers with

DDT, muttering to himself and looking pointedly at them as he did so. I am sure he caused more discomfort to the villagers than the flies, who buzzed off until he had finished, then returned.

An unexpected situation came to light during the first inspection at Liria, when I observed that some of the men had a claw inserted into the fleshy side of the hand. Andrea was unable to give any definite information as to this phenomenon, other than he thought that those so adorned were known as 'Leopard men'. I did not press the question any further, but recalled having read that a West African secret society of that name had, or still, existed some years before. At one time members of the society penetrated as far as Lui, where they were fired upon and driven off by the then missionary doctor - Dr Frazer. Another surprise, when walking along the inspection line of women, was a woman's face. I went back and looked at her more closely. One side of her nose was missing. I asked her, through Andrea's interpreting, was it the result of syphilis? She said, "No - it was leprosy."

Checking through the first results at Liria it became obvious that not all the people were making themselves available. This can be confirmed when of the new cases found less that 25% are advanced cases. I discussed this with Lolik Lado and he agreed with my conclusion and mentioned that there was a small leprosy village not too far away. He said that he would talk again with the villagers, stressing the importance of co-operation which would indicate to the government that people were interested. This resulted in several bad cases presenting themselves.

Privately, one had to be sympathetic towards those with leprosy who were often more fearful of being segregated, in a small government village, than of the disease itself. At such a village near Liria there was a dresser in charge who suffered from the disease himself, as could be seen from his badly crippled hands. He had not been properly trained and anyhow, with the extent of his deformities, he was not able to attend to treatments satisfactorily. Results of his work with the hypodermic needle could be clearly identified in the ulcerated buttocks of several patients. Out of sight - out of mind appeared to have been the policy for these villages, the Cinderellas of the medical services.

It was interesting to meet a member of Liria, who had once lived at this village. I asked him why he had left. He replied quite heatedly that he was not going back. He had spent seven years in the village and there had been no sign of improvement and he thought it had been a waste of time. Why should he stay there when there was more comfort in his home village? I explained, as best I could, that there was a new treatment available and it would, therefore, be to his advantage to return to the village. He asked when this would be. This, of course, was difficult to forecast as I was really in no position to anticipate government resolutions. (Having already suffered by a broken promise for transport.) I hazarded a guess of two years time. Fortunately, this proved accurate for within eighteen months Sulphone drugs were being used as standard treatment at these villages under the supervision of a doctor from Juba. Past agitation by Southern Sudanese chiefs had reached fruition.

Chickens were few around Liria and the opportunity of buying eggs consequently reduced. My usual breakfast omelette looked like being a thing of the past. It looked very much like tinned meat and beans would be the replacement in the immediate future. I had purchased from a Greek merchant in Juba a piece of salted bacon, so thought I would give it a try. Upon opening up the package and examining the contents, I found the bacon to consist of a lump of yellowish fat, over the face of which the lean meat showed like lines drawn with a red pencil. My natural and immediate reaction regarding the merchant's ancestry was quite a reasonable one. I did not bother to cover the bacon adequately and carried it around for the next two weeks before dumping it in the merchant's lap upon my return to Juba. I did not bother with this commodity again.

One morning, the egg situation seemed about to improve when two small boys turned up with some eggs. Dawedi identified the dozen eggs as those of guinea fowl, but was aggrieved when the boys asked what he considered to be too high a price and refused to lower their price. I looked on, mouth watering at the thought of an egg breakfast and prepared to pay the asked for price. But Dawedi, affronted by the situation and, fortunately for me, put the eggs to a test, placing them one by one in a bowl of water. Each one floated!

"Eggies bad." He pronounced with a satisfied look on his face, handing the eggs back to the prospective sellers. The boys, judging from their hurt expressions, considered Dawedi responsible for the whole rotten business.

I wrote a note to the Father at the Catholic Mission, suggesting that I examine the schoolboys at a convenient time. As an afterthought I mentioned the egg position. His return note confirmed future plans and he invited me to lunch the following day. With the note came three eggs. I accepted the invitation and not to be outdone by his generosity, sent some onions in return.

Cycling over to the school was a longer and more arduous journey than I had anticipated. The first part of the ride was over, or rather in, the clinging sandy surface of the road. At last I came to a good-surfaced dirt road, graced on either side by Paw-paw trees, which led up to the mission buildings. Dismounting at the church, I was approached by a rather nondescript individual, wearing a crumpled ill-fitting jacket and trousers. He smiled expansively in greeting, displaying several gappy teeth.

"Father Augustino?" I enquired, somewhat taken aback by his unexpected appearance.

"No, he is in the church," carefully pronounced the other, "he will be out shortly. I will tell him you are here." With this he disappeared into the church.

In a short time he reappeared with a Sudanese whom he introduced as Father Augustino. I was surprised, having expected to meet an Italian, as were the Catholic priests at Juba. We shook hands and walked to the nearby house. While final preparations for the lunch were being made, we discussed the countryside, the people, Mission school and the leprosy survey. Father Augustino spoke excellent English so we had no trouble in communicating and, so he informed me later, had been to Europe training for the priesthood. Lifting a bottle down from a high shelf, he offered me a glass of sherry. But with the temperature around a hundred degrees I diplomatically declined, for I had to cycle back to the resthouse in the hottest part of the day.

The meal began with soup, thickened with rice, followed by roast pigeon stuffed with rice. I found the predominance of rice a little too much, so spread it around the plate hoping my host would not become aware of this stratagem. But, all in vain. The third course was rice pudding; I had no choice but politely refuse outright. I left Father Augustino at three in the afternoon and eventually reached the resthouse suffering from sunburn and a touch of heartburn. The first self-inflicted as I had neglected to wear a hat.

When we examined the schoolboys at the mission we found 50 cases per thousand to have early lesions of leprosy. These results came as a surprise, when compared with those of Zanzibar (5.5 cases per thousand of the people) and Pemba (3.9 cases per thousand).

The advantage of using a bicycle was rather out-weighed by the energy lost in propelling the machine over the loose, sandy surface of the smaller roads and tracks. We found also that the inner tubes of our government issue machines were in poor condition, confirming lack of attention to their being little used. Kicking the machine may have given fleeting satisfaction but, on the negative side, damaged a foot needed for walking. During one of our frequent stops - mainly by myself - the chief reminisced on the fact that in his early days as chief he had been obliged to travel to his various villages on foot. This was no mean feat as the area where the Lokoya lived covered many miles. Perhaps this accounted for the strategic placing of wives. I managed to summon up an interest in what he said, but my thoughts were on my sorry state as we proceeded homewards after pumping up the tyres and obtaining a short-lived result. I felt shattered upon arrival at the resthouse, when I ordered up tea all round. The chief took it upon himself to repair the inner tube. I was moved by the friendly gesture and, from then on, shared my cigarettes with him. It was a small enough price to pay for his help. A better investment could not have been made, for Lolik Lado eased the way for a successful part of the Lokoya part of the survey. Social formalities completed, the chief cycled back to his village.

At this stage, due to my inexperience and the non-arrival of a water-filter from England, I had to be satisfied with hot tea as a form of refreshment. Basically, this was because local water, especially on trek, had to be boiled before drinking, as had also the water for the evening sluice down to kill off any nasty bugs lurking within. By the time I had finished my ablution I usually felt far from refreshed and a fresh shirt soaked up the pervasive sweat. Cool refreshing showers I had experienced during my short stay in Juba belonged to another life. But there was one consolation in the fact that in a couple of weeks that luxury would be available again.

Chapter 12

Ngulere - a place to remember. The village lay on a rough track at the base of the Duluba Hills, five miles from Liria and fifteen miles from Lamiega. With the absence of a resthouse, I took over the old dispensary, loathe to sleep in the open, with memories of the tales I had heard earlier at Lui, and which I did not wish to confirm personally. Inside this stuffy, square-shaped, mud-walled hut, with the main part of the room seven feet long and with six feet headroom, I put up my camp-bed and stacked my belongings. We were living, more or less, in the village itself and, throughout the day, the area was inundated with wandering goats and flies. Flies! Those persistent pests that drove one almost to breaking point, as they incessantly clustered around the eyes and mouth, seeking moisture. At Ngulere there was no respite from them from sunup to sundown, when the mosquitoes took over. Mealtimes were rather harrowing for then the flies clambered over cutlery and dishes. Only continuous fanning with the hands kept them from the food for any length of time. I covered the rim of my cup with a saucer, until the tea was cool enough to drink straight down. Apart from knowledge of their pre-feeding habit of vomiting up the contents of their stomach, my chief aversion to their presence was the sight of flies swarming over running sores on the natives' bodies. The self same flies could now be on my food. The thought sickened me and, more often than not, I pushed away food which I considered might have come in contact with them, including my tea. I cursed the heat, the flies, and whatever impulse had prompted me to take up this work.

On the outward voyage, when the ship had been negotiating

the Suez Canal, an idiosyncrasy of a fellow passenger, towards flies, now appeared to be explained. He sat opposite me one mealtime and, whilst waiting for food to appear, he spent the intervening time killing flies within his reach. Glaring about him all the while, through his monocle. The first two flies he despatched with a table-napkin, while the third he trapped under a water-glass. Extricating it with great care, he then killed it and placed the corpse with those of the others, in the centre of the table. I had found his antics highly amusing. So much so that I was obliged to leave the table to avoid laughing outright in his face. Now, in Ngulere, I could sympathise with his attitude and found the lesson a far from amusing one.

Because our survey had medical overtones, the local villagers assumed we had extensive medical knowledge. Apart from a short acquaintance with leprosy my general medical knowledge was somewhat slender. But even the administration of an aspirin went a long way to persuading the complainant that something was being done. Trivial wounds, such as a cut, were dressed by Andrea and the procedure watched with as much interest as if it were a major operation. The psychological effect having as much, if not more, curative effect than did the treatment itself. The dresser who had been in charge made himself known to us. His tattered uniform did not impress and I hoped it was not an outward expression of his ability. He explained that he had not received medical supplies for several months. I said we would notify the hospital upon our return to Juba. That is all I could promise, for I was aware that supplies were stopped for a good reason, such as when the dresser had been charging his patients for their treatment when it should have been free. But, in spite of these 'white sheep' of the medical service, there were some worthy individuals who had the welfare of their patients at heart.

It was frustrating by men such as these to be continually let down by the question of supplies, their letters requesting fresh stocks apparently shelved by the authorities. On one occasion I read a letter written by one medical assistant to the local D.C. in which, while not resorting to actual abuse, was couched in such strong terms regarding a doctor at Juba that I was glad I had seen it. I knew the doctor to whom he was referring and did not fancy the medical assistant's chances if he had received it in its present form. I suggested to him that he rewrite the letter, omitting all candid comment, however deserved it might be, and just state clearly the lack of medical supplies. I would take the letter to the D.C. myself and impress upon him the seriousness of the situation and ask him if he would notify Juba of the position. He agreed and I was able to tell the assistant that should he not receive his supplies in the near future, then he should contact the D.C.

At a nearby small village we encountered an old 'arrested' case of leprosy. An 'arrested' case is one in which the disease has left the body of its own accord or after medical treatment. Seldom does leprosy leave the body without causing some degree of disfiguration. Such cases are also referred to as 'burnt out' for the disease has, as it were, progressed through the body like a fire, before finally dying away.

Later that day, after we had returned to Ngulere, Lolik Lado asked me if I would like to go shooting guinea fowl. Of course, as I had no gun myself, this meant I would be a witness to his shooting prowess. I agreed and just before sundown, when the birds were settling down for the night on the lower branches of trees, our shooting party, consisting of the chief, sub-chief, chief's policeman (acting as gun-bearer), Andrea and myself, walked in a straggling line towards a clump of trees, where several guinea fowl were roosting. The chief and his followers were lost to view on one side of the trees as I made my way around the other. I had a fleeting memory of the episode in Pickwick Papers where Mr. Winkle was designated to shoot a rook. His companions, showing a complete lack of faith in his shooting ability, took cover. Unfamiliar with that of the chief, I wondered if I should do the same. Then came a shot and I remained unharmed. Not like Winkle's friend, Tupman, who received some shot in his arm. The chief had shot himself a brace of birds and he gave me one. My thoughts shot ahead in anticipation of a future meal.

Next day the bird was cooked in a temporary oven - a cleaned out four gallon petrol tin. The result was delicious, after my problems of food and mealtimes the previous few days. Not even flies could stop me eating that bird. I thought I would turn the occasion into a small personal celebration and follow up the main course with the remainder of a tin of fruit. Dawedi had opened this the day before, but then I had felt indisposed to eat it. Here I was unlucky, for the tin's contents were full of struggling ants. Dawedi had placed the tin in a bowl of water, but the cloth covering it had been left overhanging the edge of the bowl, bridging the water and allowing the ants access. Distended with the fowl I was not particularly worried about this and, with doubtful generosity, gave the fruit to the boys, whose taste was not so fastidious as mine.

Lamiega, our next centre for operation, was a complete contrast to Ngulere. The resthouse was well situated on the brow of a hill and overlooking a long valley, ranged on three sides by hills. The very same hills observed in the distance from Liria resthouse. What I most appreciated was that the resthouse at Lamiega was far enough away from the village to ensure a minimum of disturbance from inquisitive villagers. There were relatively few flies and, because of the altitude, there was the benefit of every small breeze. I was later to learn that these aspects were sometimes taken advantage of by people in Juba to avoid the, at times, stifling heat. For the first time since the survey began I felt capable of thinking again and I felt reasonably contented. A mood almost entirely due to being on the hill and viewing the rugged beauty of the area as a whole. It was as if I was seeing Africa for the first time. As if she were saying "Look, there is beauty as well as ugliness here."

One evening, after dark, I heard a lorry coming along the road below, then turning onto the track leading to the resthouse. I was pleasantly surprised to see Reggie Dingwall and his wife. He, in turn, expressed surprise that we had progressed so far with the survey. Our rate of progress was due to our working every day of the week and to no set hours. This procedure suited our circumstances. Jimmy Roscoe told me that in West Africa, he and a doctor worked two days and then took one day off.

The Dingwalls were a charming couple and for me, at least, their counsel and friendly demeanour will remain as a happy memory. The evening meal provided by them was a delight; iced water and fresh meat - a pleasant change from tinned foodstuffs.

The hospital truck did not arrive on time so Reggie gave Andrea and me a lift as far as Longabu, about seven miles south east of Lameiga. Here, the results of an epidemic of cerebral meningitis, eight years before, were apparent. There were few people belonging to the age groups between early teens and early twenties. These epidemics flare up now and again and little could be done under the prevailing conditions except to isolate the infected area in an attempt to prevent the disease from spreading.

At Longabu I encountered a minor case of class distinction. As I waited for the villagers to line up, with the usual happy confusion, I was approached by a native wearing long, drill slacks, shirt and trilby hat. He wished me 'Good day' and introduced himself as the village schoolmaster, adding, "These people are funny - aren't they?" Personally, I found nothing funny in the customs, or habits, of the African. Strange at times maybe, but not funny queer. So to hear a schoolmaster, who appeared to have gained in knowledge but not in wisdom, from his education, discrediting his fellows in this way moved me to anger. I made him remove his shirt and stand in line with the others. In retrospect my reason for doing this was not entirely true, but rather a combination of his remark and his air of familiarity towards me as an equal, which probably had something to do with it. He caught me at a bad moment.

As we were leaving Longabu Lolik, Lado presented me with a goat. I thanked him for it while, at the same time, feeling somewhat dubious as to the possible short term consequence of accepting the present. But, not wishing to offend, I took the beast and thanked him. Not only might there be a problem with the animal as we were moving about, but I had a nagging feeling that the goat's presence, aromatically advertised, would attract some predatory animal. With this in mind I had the cook tether the goat in the vicinity of the kitchen, some thirty yards from the resthouse. Local European opinion had it that goat flesh was well nigh indigestible. That is, if one succeeded in getting further than the chewing stage. I intended to test this theory personally when I got back to Juba, encouraged by the knowledge that medical aid would be at hand if needed.

From Lameiga we cycled to Lakoleri, which lay not far from the Luluba Hills and roughly south of Ngulere. From Lakoleri we travelled to Lomer and, as we would be spending the night there, were only taking essential items of bedding and food. Andrea and Dawedi were with me, the cook remaining behind at Lameiga resthouse with the bulk of our supplies - and the goat. Lolik Lado's party was comprised mostly of porters. He and I cycled ahead of the rest, for the early stage of the path to Lomer was well defined. Eventually we were obliged to leave our bicycles, to be collected by the porters when they came along later. We then began walking the most arduous section, the sandy bed of a dried-up stream from which clumps of rocks protruded at intervals. There was no breeze between the high rock on one side and the growth of trees or bamboo on the other. For several hours we plodded on with ever increasing discomfort in sweaty clinging clothes. At last an area of cultivation indicated that Lomer was nearby and, as we pushed past the tall stems of the dura, we came to the village.

We made our way to a tall tree at the village's centre. A group of people came to their feet to greet the chief and then myself. I was offered a deckchair, similar to the standard design, but with a skin being used instead of canvas. I sat down with a sign of relief, but then had the breath knocked out of me when the chair collapsed. There was laughter all round but all I could manage was a sickly grin as I rubbed my bruised buttocks and nursed a deflated ego. After this incident I made a practice of testing this type of chair before sitting on it. When the rest of the party arrived sometime later, I got Dawedi to brew up some tea for Lolik Lado, Andrea and myself. At the same time giving the villagers the opportunity to assemble for examination, which went off without any problems.

Later, I went to the village school, which stood a little way apart from the rest of the village. As I settled in the weather began to change. Clouds appeared overhead and the rain began to fall quite heavily. Soon, water was dripping from the thatched roof, close to the outer walls. I eased my bed back a little way in case a gust of wind blew the rain-drips inside. I noticed that the rain was dripping through the roof in several places, but fortunately none was close by. I was tired after the exertions of the day, so retired to bed early. Something disturbed me. I awoke slowly and became aware of a voice calling me accompanied by the clapping of hands. Turning my head I was surprised to see Andrea standing by the side of the bed. To my grunted enquiry as to what was the matter, he said that the chief had sent him with the message that, because of the rain, I was welcome to use one of his huts. But, as I was warm, comfortable and dry, I was reluctant to leave. So I told Andrea to thank Lolik Lado and explain that I would stay where I was.

After breakfast the following day, we examined a few people

we had missed the previous day, then prepared to retrace our steps to Lakoleri.

The plan of travel was similar to that established before, only in reverse. The chief and I rode our bicycles along a rough path until we came to the beginning of a sandy area patterned with rocks. Here we left the bicycles for the porters to bring along later. The chief gave me to understand that he knew of a short cut along the bed of a stream. After a while I began to think that it was not a short cut, as we did not appear to make progress, as we had on the outward journey. The loose sand of the stream bed hampered our passage. I carried nothing and wore upon my head a topee of large proportions which had been termed by new acquaintances, with an intended derogatory appellation of "A Missionary Helmet". I did notice afterwards that, and I believe I assumed rightly, there was only one such helmet/topee in the Sudan - and I was wearing it. At the earliest opportunity I exchanged it for a straw hat.

Lolik Lado, as usual, carried a belt of ammunition slung around his body and his rifle. In spite of these encumbrances he set a cracking pace and I was hard put to keep up with him. The walk seemed never-ending and I continually looked for landmarks but failed to recognise any. We traversed, as before on the outward journey, the sun-heated sand of dried-up streams, part over-hung with dried grass and shrubs. The reflected heat was intense and my mouth was soon dry, my feet burning and sore in my heavy shoes and clothes clung stickily to my body. Perspiration rolled down my face, from beneath my tome of a headgear, dripping down my eyebrows onto my spectacles. Blurring my vision and causing me to stumble over the uneven terrain. I could not clear my lenses for my sodden handkerchief worsened the problem by smearing the glass. As I stumbled on behind my guide I could think of nothing else but a long cool glass of water. How did the chief feel? I didn't ask. It was rather unnerving to watch his unfaltering progress. Still, I thought, if he can keep it up - so can I, even though I would gladly have lain down for a long rest. At last we came to the base of the hills and the knowledge that our destination was not far away gave me added strength.

At the village we both collapsed into deckchairs (I was too tired to check its worthiness) beneath some trees and a woman brought the chief some water to drink. I watched him enviously as he gulped down the water and sent the woman for more. But to risk a 'Jippy Tummy' by drinking unboiled water was not worth it, so I watched and drooled at the mouth. An hour or so later when the main party arrived, Dawedi made one of the best brews of tea I had ever tasted.

By mid-afternoon the expected lorry from Juba had not arrived as arranged. Tired of sitting around just waiting, I decided that I might just as well return to the Lamiega resthouse, where I could wash and change my clothes. Telling the others to wait for the lorry, I cycled off alone. The road wound its way up into the hills and then, at last, I reached the intersection where the track led up to the resthouse. As I turned the corner I was almost run into by a lorry. The driver was a Scotsman attached to the Agriculture Department and whom I had met on a previous occasion, though not in such dangerous circumstances. I must have looked a rather disreputable individual, wearing a sweat-covered expression and stained clothing. He raised his eyebrows and asked, "Where in the hell have you been?"

"Are you going to Juba?" I countered.

"Yes - do you want a lift?"

"Just try and stop me." I replied both quickly and thankfully. Slinging my bicycle aboard, I climbed into the cab.

What blessed luck! Another three or four hours and I would be in Juba, luxuriating under a shower and having a cool drink. In the meantime, I scrounged a drink from my driver. On the way to Juba we stopped at Lakoleri, where and when I told Andrea and Dawedi that I was going on ahead to Juba. As it did not seem that the lorry from Juba would be coming that day, I suggested they kill the goat that evening and bring the carcase back to Juba with them. As it turned out we met the lorry some miles down the road. I told the driver where to find Andrea and Dawedi. It did not get back to Juba until the following morning having, I suspect, missed the ferry.

The goat was killed, so I was told, but seemed to have gone "bad" immediately and had to be thrown away. I wondered in whose direction it had been thrown.

Chapter 13

Juba was the reception and distribution centre of news in the Southern Sudan; arriving by air, river and road. It was continually supplemented by an unending stream of people travelling from one place to another within the territory. Finally to be circulated through gossip at dinner parties etc.

The social scale at Juba could be roughly gauged by observing the placement of buildings. The Governor's residence, on the outskirts of town, was the pinnacle of social standing, while the other houses, between there and the centre of town, were roughly allocated in order of precedence. Juba resthouse, while situated on the opposite side of the road to that of the Governor, had no social significance. It was positioned for the convenience of travellers. I myself was eventually to use it on a regular basis and, by so doing met only a few outside the scope of my work.

I never attended the weekly play-reading sessions, though I heard they were quite good, preferring the solitary company of books. Sunday evening was a musical evening. On the one occasion when I attended, at the house of the Game Warden, Colonel Malloy, I rather concluded, after a short while, that I had made a mistake by allowing myself to be persuaded to attend. I sat in bored silence for most of the time for, at that period, my appreciation of the classics had not been established. Looking around at the gathering, as they stared at each other with unseeing eyes, lost to the music, or sat with closed eyes, I rather wished I was in the bush, listening to the more primitive sounds of drums and singers*.

After their early afternoon rest, tennis enthusiasts made their way to the hard courts behind the Juba Hotel. But the most welcome feature was the hotel's swimming pool. To enjoy it cost 4 piastres and tickets were obtained from a small boy, who was always hovering nearby. One day I had an opportunity of studying this particular lad at close quarters as he searched his pockets for change. His turban had slipped away from his forehead and a tuberculoid lesion of leprosy was clearly visible. I must have stared at him too intently for, after giving me the change, he hurried away and I never saw him again. No doubt he was aware of my profession and was afraid that he might be sent to Luri Rokwe.

Luri Rokwe was six miles north of Juba on the Terakeka road. I first visited the village when, at the time, it could hardly be considered as a place where those suffering from leprosy could stay. The huts were overcrowded and the general layout left much to be desired. Sanitation - an all-important feature in the prevention of disease, was practically non-existent. There was only one latrine for eighty patients - and that situated on the far side of the village, amid the crops. This meant that patients on the other side of the village, furthest away from the latrine, did not always bother to use it, using instead the waste ground near their huts. And while modern methods of treatment for leprosy had been practised at Lui, Luri Rokwe, in common with other smaller district villages under Government supervision, was still using Hydnocarpus Oil as standard treatment. What made this the more scandalous was that the village was only a short distance from

---

* But this was before I had experienced them at night for an indefinite period.

Juba, so that supervised treatments would not have been too inconvenient*.

While Juba resthouse was away from the main part of the town, on the whole I found the comparative seclusion welcome, even though at times it meant a walk of a mile or so to shops and offices. Ten piastres - 20p - was the charge per night. Your own boys looked after you, as usual, for the duties of the gaffir (caretaker) were confined to looking after the building and keeping it clean. Duties which were not always carried out to the letter. The resthouse was a large one, with a communal kitchen, a pantry and a large dining room. The latter rarely used for its intended purpose, but as an extra bedroom. There were three small bedrooms and, at the end of the passageway leading to these, near the showers, were two toilets. These were composed of a wall-to-wall box with a central toilet seat. On the floor nearby was the ubiquitous item of toilet ware - the sandbox. The contents of which were sprinkled over your contribution when finished. Beneath the seat, to receive natural waste, was a bucket. Access to this was through a flap to the outside, making it accessible to the 'Bucket-men' who removed the old and substituted the new. This function was carried out after dark using a lorry with no lights. It was as though the authorities, in deference to the European population, were keeping hidden the fact that white people also had bodily functions. During a break at a dinner party, or drinks evening, the inside toilet was taken over by the women, while the men used the garden in which to relieve themselves. This, of course, applied to micturition only.

---

* This situation must have improved at the same time as that of the Lirian village.

A weeks stay in Juba gave me a chance to recover some of the composure I had lost on the first leg of my survey. It was suggested that I should perhaps have a break inasmuch as the inhabitants of Juba could be examined. There were still problems with transport. We examined first Malakia - the native quarter. This lay on sloping ground between the centre of Juba and the Nile. It was the collection of buildings I had seen when I first arrived at Juba. The huts of the quarter were circular with mud walls and thatched roofs. Some were larger than those in outside villages. Several brick-built latrines were available for the occupants of the huts and the heavy aroma emanating from them confirmed their constant use. The huts were rented to the people by the Government and, while they might be registered under one name, they were invariably crowded with visiting relatives and friends. The population here was a mixed one, made up from several tribes - Azande, Bari, Fejelu, Lokoya, Nyambura and Moru, with a sprinkling of Dinka and some Northern Sudanese.

Examinations were held in the late afternoon as most of the men were at work until then. The time was also convenient for the women. Thus it was only possible to work for two or three hours before the light was insufficient for a proper examination. The people were inspected in roughly constructed lean-to, open-topped shelters of bamboo and grass, or in their own houses, which was usually the case with northerners who, with few exceptions, had far better housing conditions. Under a hot sun, a confined working area and the close proximity of perspiring bodies, the atmosphere was overpowering at times. On most days I was relieved to finish. It was not unusual to find women wearing one dirty skirt over another, while the record was held by one woman who wore six skirts. Similarly, some of the men wore a dirty old pair of shorts beneath a comparatively clean pair. This contrasted with the dress adopted by visitors to the town who retained their mode of dress seen in the villages.

Juba had an incidence of 32 cases of leprosy per thousand of those examined. I became aware that in Juba, at least, I had acquired the name of "Doctor of the Bloody People". Obviously based upon the appearance of the disease bearing a reddish-bronze colour. I was informed of this by John Hannah the A.D.C. at Juba.

Leaving Juba for the second time, to complete the survey of Lolik Lado's area, I found that most of the glamour and expectancy of my first trip had dwindled significantly, tempered by my initial experiences. The resthouse was similarly located as that of Lamiega, on the top of a hill and a short distance from the village of Gerenia. Up to then I had been wearing shorts and shirt but here, where it rained most of the time, I found it more comfortable to wear khaki slacks and a windcheater to keep warm. The coolness experienced brought some relief inasmuch it tended to rejuvenate the system after the previous heat.

The chief was staying at a village a mile or so down the road, so Andrea and I cycled there. The lorry, as usual having gone back to Juba. Up to this time we had experienced no real problems with our work, but here it came from an unexpected quarter. A schoolboy, home on holiday from a Catholic school and, having been obliged to wear a uniform as part of his schooling, he was loathe to remove his clothes for examination. In spite of the fact that all others present were naked. His refusal brought him into an argument with the chief and I saw the chief's anger rising as the lad refused his order. I was not prepared for what happened next when the chief's policeman stepped forward and administered two sharp strokes of his hide whip across the lad's buttocks. The lad then reluctantly undressed. I did not interfere. To have done so would have undermined the chief's authority.

So that my face would not show my mixed feelings, I looked down at my notepad and busied myself with making a drawing of the policeman. Absorbed in this, and unknown to me, I had an audience of small boys, one of whom pointed in the direction of my model, then laughed. I quickly put the drawing away. Just as we finished the work there I felt an urgent need to respond to a call of nature. The immediate vicinity was bereft of cover, but there was a large anthill about two hundred yards away which would give adequate privacy. I began walking towards the anthill only to stop when I realised that I was accompanied by a crowd of young boys, obviously intent on witnessing what I would do next. Hurriedly, I explained to Andrea where and why I was going and he prevailed upon the boys to remain where they were. Fortunately the anthill was adequate in every way to cover my activities and I returned trying to look unconcerned.

When I added milk to my tea, shortly after we had returned to the resthouse, I found lumps floating on its surface. I shouted for Dawedi to make some more. This he did with the same result. I then realised that troops in the North African desert, during the war, had had the same experience and found it due to the mineral content in the well water. Obviously the same thing was happening here. So I had cocoa instead, with sugar to disguise any taste.

A species of grey-mottled 'horse' fly was a plague in this particular section of the track, which was steep, so that we were obliged to dismount and push our machines to the top of the slope. It was then that we were attacked by the flies who came at us from all directions. Defend as we might, we invariably lost the encounter, even though we might have killed two or three flies at a time, it was they who drew first blood. Cycling to a nearby village we encountered flies everywhere. They seemed to have some sort of bush telegraph alerting our impending arrival. Every time I was bitten, a shiver ran down my back and I tensed myself in anticipation of further bites. Too much of that sort of thing could have had me twitching like a horse's hindquarters. What made the situation worse was that the road, leading to the village, was dotted with rock-hard anthills and scarred with deep ruts. An ungodly combination which we frantically tried to avoid, in addition to swotting flies. Usually these and tsetse fly are found in game country. Later, I mentioned the problem to a vet, who suggested that they had probably been left behind by a herd of buffalo. If they could penetrate a buffalo skin what chance did we have?

One night the camp-bed broke and I had to make an emergency repair with string until I could get back to town. A not very successful operation on my part as the bed nearly collapsed when I first tried it, leaving me in a state of apprehension during the night.

Those who have had to resort to the use of a pit latrine will appreciate my feeling of uneasiness when I had occasion to use one unfamiliar to me and so an unknown quantity. Resthouse latrines were never inspected regularly and, I suppose, the authorities concerned relied on complaints by the users before rectifying any deficiencies. The latrine at Gerenia was fifteen yards from the resthouse. It was on the small size, with a low roof and a doorway not more that five feet in height, through which one entered in a crouching position. To a great extent this position was maintained inside, as it was not possible to stand to your full height. In the centre of the hardened dirt floor was a hole, about four inches in diameter, covered by a flat stone. Consequently, with this limited entry to the latrine, it was rather a hit and miss affair. Assuming a position similar to that of a Sumo wrestler, to be really successful in this procedure it helped if you had strong legs, a good eye and very good timing. The circular wall of loosely packed bamboo was covered by the tunnels of white ants which every time I entered set up a furious rustling to warn me off. I broke open one of the tunnels and pushing a stem of dried grass inside, extracted an angry ant, clinging tightly to the grass with its over-developed pincer, which comprised the larger part of its head. The next day I saw the damaged tunnel had been repaired.

Later, in Juba, I was shown a number of bottled specimens of the white ant, ranging from a 4" long Queen with a highly polished body, bulging with eggs, to the workers who cared for her and were only a fraction of her size. The Queen lived in a Royal Chamber, together with the King whose prime reason for living was to fertilise the eggs. Food was not eaten and then immediately digested, but passed through the ants several times until every vestige of nourishment had been extracted, the final use for the residue that of plastering the wall of the nest. An entomologist suggested to me that an effective way of getting rid of white ants was to exploit this facet of their feeding habits. He said that a piece of corrugated cardboard, soaked in a solution of water and crushed mepacrine was irresistible to the ants. Those foraging would eat the bait and become constipated. Unable to excrete, the feeding system was broken and eventually the community would die out. At the time I was inclined to consider this more of a theory than a practical solution. But later I heard from another source that the method worked. The entomologist's further suggestion that a gallon of old sump oil poured around the wooden supports of buildings to deter white ants was more feasible.

One rainy morning the D.C.'s lorry arrived and the driver handed me a note to the effect that the D.C. and his party would be waiting for us at the junction of the Gerenia/Nimule roads. At the meeting place I changed over to the luxury of a saloon car. With Reggie Dingwall was his wife and John Hannah. The former was on his way to Lobonok, to hold court, and was taking me along to introduce me to the chief of that area and make arrangements for a future survey.

We spent the first night in a resthouse, the second in the open near a Sudan Medical Service dispensary. A mile from the dispensary, and not far from the main road, was a government leprosy village. It was in the usual shocking state that I had come to expect. When Andrea and I inspected the place we found that treatment for the patients was, to all intents and purposes, non-existent, apart from oil injections being given by a crippled dresser. This state of affairs was due to the fact that this particular area was only accessible by road for a month in the year. But this excuse for the condition of the village hardly held water when the S.M.S.

dispensary was but a short distance away and where there appeared to be adequate stocks of medicines etc. There were not more than a dozen patients in the village, ranging from a toothless grannie to a babe-in-arms. The people told me they were unable to bury their dead because of a lack of necessary tools to break the hard ground. They were also short of hoes for the purpose of cultivation.

Their requests did not appear unreasonable and I mentioned their needs to Reggie Dingwall, together with their problem of an adequate water supply. People in their weakened condition could not be expected to travel any great distance for this basic necessity. In some areas the problem of water in the dry season was a serious one. Women and girls were obliged to travel miles in their trip to a water-hole. Should the source be a stagnant pool, used for the joint purposes of washing and drinking, it was a potential breeding ground for disease.

Later that day we drove five miles to the Nile and, leaving the car at the near bank, crossed the river in a dug-out canoe to Lobonok. The crossing was a weird process for it was virtually impossible to cross the river directly, due to the swift-flowing current. On the side where we embarked an eddy passed along the bank against the direction taken by the rest of the river. This took us upstream, until suddenly the two crew swung the canoe into the mainstream and we went rapidly in the opposite direction downstream. The paddlers swung their craft across stream and began paddling in what must be described as a frenzy. We eventually reached the opposite bank but well away from our intended landing place. But then, one of nature's wonders, another eddy, similar to the first, took us back upstream to our destination.

This was the only spot for miles where the Nile could be crossed with any degree of surety. I wonder who was the first to discover this freak of nature and was it the reason for the siting of Lobonok.

We met the chief at the courthouse, a low-walled thatch-roofed building, with a raised central square, upon which the chief sat to hear the cases. I understood nothing of what was going on so left the stifling atmosphere in the building at the earliest opportunity. I returned to the river's edge and waited for Reggie and Mrs. Dingwall.

The next day we returned to Juba.

Chapter 14

South of Juba, near Rejaf, was a rather remarkable monument. Known to Europeans as the 'Baker Stone', after Sir Samuel Baker, who had explored extensively in the area. It was known to the Bari as the 'Gore Stone', in honour of one of their early chiefs. The stone had either been placed on a giant ant-hill, or the earth had been cut away to leave it high on a compact column of earth. It was a massive piece of stone; thirty feet long, twenty-five feet wide and, at its largest end, six feet thick. I asked the local chief about its history. He volunteered the information that, at one time in the past, it had been used for sacrificial purposes, goats being killed. There were several holes the diameter of a clenched fist, reaching downwards in the earthen column. In these holes had been placed gifts and money to please the gods. Or was it a scam by a witch-doctor? Nearby was a small cemetery containing headstones, the majority of which bore French names, for at one time the French had a military post here.

In the New Year we were working west of the Juba-Meredi road. We had set up at a village school close to the road and from there it seemed appropriate to visit the village of Gorom, the following day. When this plan was explained to the locals, from whose number we would be needing porters for the proposed journey, an animated discussion broke out between the chief and the villagers. On enquiring the reason for the dispute, they explained that on the same route to Gorom a man had been killed by a buffalo the previous day. Did they think it would be too dangerous to proceed? This was affirmed. Should I send to Juba for a game-scout? There was an emphatic 'Yes'. Of course they would - it was an opportunity for them to have fresh meat. And I, the newcomer/innocent was conveniently playing their game. I sent a note to Juba explaining the situation as I saw it and asking for a game-scout to accompany us. But next morning, when no one had turned up, we were forced to leave without him.

Game-scouts came under the jurisdiction of Colonel Malloy, the Province Game Warden, whose headquarters in Juba were not far from the resthouse. Apart from ensuring that there was no poaching in the Game Reserve, the scouts dealt with any dangerous animals who had been responsible for loss of life and would, in all probability continue to do so. Deaths of people, or domestic stock, were often the result of inaccurate shooting by amateurs, or because the guns used were of the wrong calibre. So the wounded animal would escape the hunter but, disabled, would be unable to hunt for food as before and so, the animal, usually a lion, kills domestic animals or, at worse becomes a man-eater. In this sort of situation game-scouts are called in to despatch it.

At first, when the game-scout I had asked for did not appear, and because of the demonstration put on by the villagers earlier, I felt a little nervous, to say the least. However, when I decided that we should leave, the porters seemed to accept the situation and moved out singing and carrying various bundles upon their heads. This gave me a degree of comfort and confidence for, if they were singing, it could not be all that dangerous. But what I did not know then was that making a noise, particularly at night, was the natives' way of letting any animals know they were coming. This ploy was really the best they could come up with. As we were leaving I was handed a long stick. For defence? It looked quite inadequate under the circumstances. But 'No', it was to brush aside the tall grasses we would encounter on the first section of our journey. In places it reached up to my shoulders. Good cover, I thought for a hot-under-the-horn buffalo? Still unseen by us, the porters were still singing up ahead. As the grass became shorter, so polished stalks made walking difficult as my leather-soled shoes slid about, causing me to stumble frequently, so that now I was pleased to use the stick as a support. The bare-footed porters, up ahead and in view now, had no such problem.

Then came the throbbing of drums from behind us, to be faintly answered from some place ahead. Possibly a nervous reaction but I had a sudden desire to laugh, when I recalled the early films I had seen of people on safari. Now I was here in a similar situation but, whereas the drums in the films were a portent of something sinister and threatening, in this instance it was just one village getting in touch with another.

The country became more open, dotted with small clumps of thorn trees and, over this rather barren-looking aspect were scattered patches, looking like sites of small fires. The dust was whitish-grey in colour, streaked with blue-black. The ground was becoming scorchingly hot and dragging feet (mine) caused small clouds of dust to rise. Even the porters had stopped singing. Rocks and trees blurred in the waves of heat rising from the ground.

About half-way to Gorom we stopped in the dried-up bed of a stream. Not entirely dried-up for there was a small pool of water near one of the banks, in the shade of an overhanging tree. The porters ignored the liquid, to call it water would give it a quality contrary to its unappetising appearance. Instead they scraped a depression in the sand, not far from the pool and soon the filtered water came through in a condition more suited for drinking, although its flavour would not have been to everyone's taste. I had some water in a flask so had no worries over quenching my thirst. In most dry river-beds, in the dry season, these attempts to find water are made both by man and beast.

After five hours walking we came to Goram, to find that the man who had been killed by the buffalo was being buried near the village. Goram itself was deserted as all the villagers had gone to the burial. I did not see the actual burial but many graves were constructed on the same principle. The normal deep trench was dug and then a 'shelf' was cut out on one side, on which the body was placed. The identification of graves varies with different tribes and with the status of that person within the tribe. Moru graves have stones over them, while the Bongo tribe have stones, piled together in a heap, together with a carved wooden post set among the stones. For the Mandari, a rough framework of wooden poles sufficed. The arrangement of stones over a Moru grave indicated whether the person buried was an adult or a child. If a child, several small upright stones supported a larger, flat stone on top. An adult's grave consisted of a large, flat stone, leaning at an angle, and supported by a smaller. In addition, if the stone inclined to the East, the grave was that of a woman, to the West, it was that of a man.

After taking over the village school as our headquarters at Gorom, it was a relief to remove my sweat-soaked shirt and shoes. Stripped to my underpants and enjoying a wash, I heard a subdued whisper. Glancing up, I saw half-a-dozen young girls seated at the other end of the building. I motioned for them to leave. One said something to her companions and they all laughed. I made a step towards them and they ran off giggling. Shortly afterwards a young boy came along, his hand supported by a rough sling. He explained that he had been stung by a scorpion. There was nothing we could do for him medically, but a cup of well-sweetened tea gave him some degree of consolation. As he sat near us, drinking his tea, some of the villagers remarked upon the fact that 'He was having tea with the white man'.

Those villagers available we examined later that afternoon. One interesting aspect of this examination was that one of the cases of leprosy identified was a former patient at Lui. A young mother who had to leave when she became pregnant. Andrea said that her condition had deteriorated since she had left. Reasons for patients leaving, or having to leave, varied. I came across such a case when I was at Lui, when a man who had left the colony before I took over (while the Roscoes were on leave) returned, expressing the wish to continue treatment. When I asked the reason for his leaving he said that he had left to look after his parents who were both blind. His story was confirmed by Elase and so he was treated as an out-patient. His condition was not really serious and, as he lived but a short distance from Lui, he was able to attend for treatment once a week.

After the end of our late afternoon inspection, I was completing my notes, sat in the shade, while Andrea went off with the sub-chief to have a drink. I heard voices raised a short distance away. Then became aware of a slapping sound. Looking up I saw, in the centre of a small group of men, a completely naked man jumping up and down. The slapping sound was being made by his long penis hitting against his stomach. He shouted out to attract attention, pointing at himself as he jumped in the air. I did not understand the comments he was making, perhaps it was just as well. If Andrea had been there I would have suggested that the exhibitionist stopped, before he beat himself to death. [And this, in all probability, would have ended his capers.]

At dawn the next day there was a mournful wailing in the village. I left my bed to find out the cause of the noise. Andrea explained that the wailing was being made by the sister of the man buried the previous day. It was customary she do this for a week or more, after the burial. I did hear of one exception to this custom. An old woman living near Lui turned up as a professional mourner, whenever there was a death at the CMS hospital there. Performing cartwheels and other gymnastics in the hospital grounds.

When we were preparing to leave Gorom, Andrea said the porters wanted to see me. I met them and asked what was the problem. They said they wished to be paid for their labour before they started on the return trip. I had visions of trouble. Then I had a thought.

"Tell them I never pay for eggs before the hen lays them." I saw them thinking this over, so continued

"Neither will I pay for work before it is done."

The porters looked at each other when Andrea translated my message. Then, to my relief, they laughed and picked up their loads and set off, soon to be singing once more.

I reached the end of the return walk in a state of exhaustion, feeling sick and with a raging thirst. While the cook made tea I contented myself with resting in a deckchair.

That afternoon the lorry arrived from Juba and took us to the next village. The walk from Gorom had resulted in a patch of skin being rubbed off one of my toes. That evening I had little sleep and throughout the night it throbbed unceasingly. I was thankful when morning came. The foot was now beginning to swell and it was obvious that infection had set in. Because of this the day seemed unbearingly long, but the monotony of general examinations was broken at one village, where we examined several young Bari girls who had been through a form of initiation. Their bodies had been cut and then ashes rubbed into the wounds, which would eventually result in raised weals on the skin. Already the designs were standing out with some prominence. In addition to this, several teeth had been removed to encourage fertility. This resulted in the girls' mouths being held tightly by a cord which ran around the head. Blood seeped out from the corner of their lips. One of the girls blew a whistle as we approached, a warning to males that, at this stage of their initiation, discourse with the girls was forbidden. However, the chief, sub-chief, Andrea and I were allowed into the compounds, where the girls were temporarily housed. As the youngest girl put her cloth between her thighs so that we might inspect her upper limbs, she grimaced with pain. It was then that I realised the girls had also been circumcised, so we relaxed this part of the examination with the others.

Returning to Juba that day, I showed my foot to Dr Wheaton. He in turn asked his surgeon to look at it. He grimaced and had a few words with Dr Wheaton. This resulted in my staying with Dr Wheaton for five days 'So that he could keep an eye on it'. During the latter part of the week Andrea called to inform me that my cook was in prison. He was not coming out for some time either. The police had found, upon arresting him for drunkenness, that he was in possession of government property, namely my bicycle, and was an escaped prisoner from Yei District Prison. I did two things. Made Dawedi cook, to his great delight, and sent to the Juba police to get my ex-cook's uniform back.

When I left Dr Wheaton's I was fortunate to obtain accommodation, for several days, at the house of the CMS accountant and his wife. He being the source of my salary from BELRA. On the second day I was there, while resting on a settee, there was a sudden pain in my infected foot. It then hit my knee and finally my groin. This sequence occurred every five minutes or so. I waited until my hosts' siesta was over, then asked them to contact a doctor. When he arrived he looked casually at the foot, then suggested I go the hospital for tests. He made the obvious enquiries as to how the foot had become infected and then, out of the blue, asked if I had been with any native women. Wrong-footed by this unexpected and unnecessary question, I paused with my reply of 'No'. Afterwards I thought I should have asked him what I'd been using for intercourse - my TOE!

The second night I was in hospital the native assistant, seeing I was in pain, asked me if I would like some morphine. Willing to try anything which would ease the pain, I said 'Yes'. But it gave little relief. The next morning a nursing sister stormed into the ward demanding to know why I had asked for morphine. I told her that it had been offered to me by an assistant. She went off, with feathers ruffled, and I never saw her nor the doctor again. Neither was I offered treatment. The following afternoon I got out of bed and went along to the office, determined to find out what was going on. There was no one there, but on the desk was a patients' record book. Open, and with my name prominently displayed. There was a comment beneath it:

'Probably thinks it to be worse than it is.'

I stood there for a short period seething with rage. It was obvious I had been expected to read the comment. So I left.

The Irish couple explained they were unable to offer me accommodation as the room was needed for someone else. I accepted this, but thought that maybe it was because my foot was beginning to smell. I couldn't blame them. I went to the resthouse, which meant it would be less convenient to get to the hospital, to have my dressing changed every day. Later that week, while at the hospital having my dressing changed, the doctor of earlier acquaintance strolled by. Falsely smiling with his teeth and exaggerating his air of pomposity he said, in passing,

"Still having trouble again?"

I answered with a brief "Yes". But my true thoughts were both obscene and undoubtedly libellous.

Occasionally, I managed to arrange transport to nearby villages and became more mobile myself, by wearing a loosely tied sandal on my left foot. Then, just as I was beginning to think that things were improving, I developed a boil in one of my arm-pits. This nuisance did not plague me for long, for I managed to remove the core in a short time.

The foot continued to weep at times, which restricted the distance I could walk.

Chapter 15

The dry season reaches its peak in January and from the northern desert wastes blows a persistent, though at times almost imperceptible wind, bringing with it black smuts from bush fires and a scorching heat. Road surfaces are thickly coated with dust which, at the passing of vehicles, rises chokingly to billow slowly skywards, before settling once more. The metalwork of the lorry becomes unbearably hot and the act of resting one's forearm out of the cab window, for coolness, may result in unexpected sun-burn. You experience the sensation of moisture drying on your lips, as they crinkle with the heat. The draught of hot air into the cab makes your eyes dry and smart, while the necessity to inhale dries the membranes of your nose. Shirt and shorts become saturated with perspiration, but dry just as quickly in the sun.

On the east bank of the Nile lived the Bilinya tribe; rather more isolated than other tribes as they were away from main roads and the river. One of their greatest needs was medical treatment and from this particular area we brought back more people requiring hospitalisation than from any other. This somewhat detached pocket of people had an extremely high incidence of leprosy - over 61 cases per thousand people.

Sometimes we entered a hut to see someone who was too old to travel to the examination point, or because the occupant was ill. In the huts over-crowding was rife, both with people and their possessions. The air was hot and fouled by smoke from the fire burning on the floor of the hut.

The road closely followed the river once out of this area and, as the locality was part of the Game Reserve, we saw a variety of animals during the course of our travels. For me there was the thrill of seeing buffalo for the first time, grazing on an open patch of ground, several hundred yards from the road. From inside the cab they could not be seen, but we were made aware of them by the shouts of our passengers. Halting the lorry, I climbed on top of the cab to get a better view. From where we were they looked huge, standing out sharp and black against a back-ground of green. Several of the group turned to face us and there was a clear view of their large heads and sweeping horns. Tails began to twitch and, not being conversant with the reason for this, I supposed it not to be akin to the friendly gesture of a dog. Having, a month before, been appraised of the damage which could be done to a vehicle by an aggressive buffalo, I told the driver to continue our journey. The passengers were disappointed, seeing their hope of fresh meat fading. My own disappointment lay in the fact that I did not have a camera, so determined that this would be rectified on my next visit to Juba.

After I had purchased a camera - a folding Brownie - I did not see hide nor hair of a buffalo at the locale again. However, on the same stretch of road I had seen some ostrich, on open ground between the road and the Nile. I turned to the ostrich for photographic expression. When an opportunity arose, in between our work schedule, I stopped under some trees and then, using what cover was available, walked slowly towards them. A short distance ahead, in fairly open ground, was an ant-hill. It looked an ideal piece of cover so, indicating to the others to remain where they were, I dropped to the ground and began crawling, in the approved fashion, over some elbow and knee-pricking growth. Soon perspiring heavily from my efforts, my goal seemed further away than I had anticipated. Then it was in front of me and behind its shelter I paused to catch my breath. I wasn't taking any risk of camera shake. Having made the necessary adjustments to the camera I edged out slowly around the ant-hill. The ostrich had gone! Well, almost, I caught a brief flash of their yellow legs as they disappeared into cover. No burying of heads in the ground, or sand, here. Disappointed, I stood up and turning around I saw the reason for my failure. Both Andrea and Dawedi were standing in full view but a few yards away, obviously having misinterpreted my signals. What they must have thought as they walked behind me I could only guess. Their facial expressions gave nothing away. They may have considered I had been carrying out some strange part of a European hunting ritual, or, have put it down to another of my idiosyncratic traits.

On one sector of the road the bush on either side was criss-crossed with elephant tracks, the animals' passage further confirmed by the large number of small trees which had been uprooted, while branches from the larger trees had been ripped off, leaving fresh white scars on their trunks. The area looked as if it had been hit by a cyclone and giving evidence that animals, as well as man, are capable of destroying their environment. The elephants appeared to use this route during the hours of darkness, for we never saw them during the daytime, just their devastation and dung, the latter steaming in the early morning sun. Buck and gazelle were occasionally seen. Once we started up a gazelle which had been crouching by the side of the road. It raced alongside the lorry for a few seconds before, with a sudden burst of speed, it cut across in front of the bonnet and soon disappeared. At the time we were travelling in the region of thirty miles per hour.

The importance of Mongalla to me was that it had a resthouse. On the minus side was its closeness to the Nile and therefore the presence of ubiquitous mosquitoes at night. When I had finished my usual wash-down in a canvas 'bath', I put on my pyjamas, on top of which I wore drill slacks and a dressing gown. Not having the luxury of mosquito boots, I tucked my trousers into a pair of canvas boots. This rigmarole was concluded with the application of a concoction supplied by Juba hospital as a mosquito deterrent, but which proved to have little effect. The ointment was messy and its oil base made clothing and bedding filthy. Sitting close to the oil lamp, trying to read, meant tolerating the hordes of gyrating insects attracted by the light. But the main distraction was from bats and their tendency to land on my shoulders. At first I tended to pause before brushing them off, but eventually just shrugged them off. At least they were not bloodsuckers, as were the mosquitoes.

I slept in the open, a few yards away from the resthouse, to enjoy the benefit of any breeze. In the light of the moon I could see the silhouettes of dozens of mosquitoes clinging to the outside of the net, all probing hopefully for entry. The net had to be positioned around the bed before sundown so that the insects could not conceal themselves in the bedding, to emerge later to kiss you goodnight, in their own inimitable fashion. Even with the most careful precautions some would succeed in breaking through the screen, so that it was the practice by some to spray the net and bedding before retiring. A trek-bed is not very wide and when the night is hot and humid clothes are often thrown off, allowing bare arms and legs to rest against the sides of the net, where the proboscis of the mosquito awaits. One morning I awoke to find the net full of mosquitoes, their bellies bloated with my blood. My arms and face were covered with bites some of which, on the back of one of my hands, were so close together that they made one solid raised patch. I took Paludrine tablets every day and these undoubtedly prevented my getting malaria although, not all mosquitoes are carriers of the disease.

Several hundred yards away from the resthouse were some tall palms and, while taking a short walk one morning, I saw a group of bats resting among the branches, large eyes glowing in the morning sun.

Few people were living in the immediate area and the only buildings of consequence were half a dozen native huts and a small shop. A new brick-built shop was in the course of construction, most certainly at the behest of an enterprising local merchant. Work on the building was being carried out by several Dinka. The tribe are taller than most other people in the South Sudan, most adults being well over six feet in height, of slim build and with long arms and legs. When resting in the standing position the men placed a foot on the opposite knee, while supported by their spear. Most were near naked, with little pretence at covering. They are herdsmen and obsessed with cattle, so it was not unexpected to find that they should compare a white man to a bull and a white woman to a cow, both additionally bearing a reference to the person's habits. A District Commissioner, who was in the habit of holding court under a large tree was named 'The-Black-Bull-who-Sits-

Under-The-Tree', the first part of his name indicative of his temper, the second of his habit. A CMS nurse went under the name of 'The-Fat-White-Cow'. This allusion to her plumpness did nothing for her ego, nor did the reference to a 'cow', which could be taken in its derogatory context.

While, on the surface, the Dinka might appear to be a rather placid type of individual, this assumption was somewhat erased in 1952, when there was a terrible battle between dissenting groups over a cattle stealing incident. A hundred tribesmen were wounded in the affray, some killed. About half the wounded were brought down-river to Juba hospital where the resident surgeon had a hectic few days sewing up gaping spear wounds. It took the combined efforts of two doctors to remove a spear embedded in one man's mouth, one doctor holding the man's head, while the other tugged with both hands to release the weapon. The poor wretch must have suffered agony on the trip down-river and its aftermath.

After we had unloaded our gear in the resthouse we drove to several nearby villages to inform people that we would be examining them shortly. One of the villages, south of Mongalla, contained a number of local Mandari, together with several from other tribes. They were engaged in catching fish and then salting them, ready for collection by the Juba merchant who employed them. At the rear of the huts a large amount of gutted fish lay on long trestles, drying in the sun. Even the large amount of salt sprinkled on the fish did not deter the swarming flies. Just across from the river-bank was a small island and between the two the fishermen stretched a net. I asked the foreman if he had any fresh fish to spare. He said there were none at present, but he promised me a fish the following day.

Early next morning, to my surprise, a man arrived from the village, with two large fish (probably Nile Perch) for which he refused payment. After thanking the man, I gave the fish to Dawedi to cook for the afternoon meal.

Returning to Mongalla later that day, I saw Dawedi crouching over the kitchen fire. I went over to him.

"Food ready, Dawedi?" I enquired.

"Five minutes." said Dawedi, giving his stock reply.

I noticed he was holding a frying pan over the fire and in the pan a dark mass of rather indeterminate shape simmered in a dark liquid. From time to time the liquid heaved itself reluctantly into bubbles. The action intrigued me. I pointed to this mystery of the Dawedi cuisine. "What's that?"

"Fish." Dawedi replied, probing the contents of the pan with a fork.

This reply was totally unexpected and for a moment I was lost for words. A piece of the outer crust fell away from the brown mass, exposing something vaguely resembling fish. I had mixed feelings regarding this concoction so asked Dawedi what he had used in the cooking.

Dawedi frowned for a moment and then spat out "Blist!"

"Blist?" Now I was worried. "Show me what you used."

Dawedi went to the stores and, to my relief, came back with a packet of Bisto. I tried the fish and hurriedly got rid of it. If there were words to describe it, I had yet to come across them. I told Dawedi to throw it away and boil up some more. Dawedi shook his head at my fastidiousness.

An hour later, Dawedi signified that my late lunch was ready. I seated myself, hungry and expectant, at the table. The ground-nut soup was excellent, as always; then came the fish. The newly boiled section was there - next to the Bistoed fish. I raised my eyes heavenwards as Dawedi scuffed back to the kitchen. The newly boiled fish was full of bones. I rejected the meal and Dawedi removed it, making clicking noises with his tongue as he walked slowly back to his kitchen. I opened a tin of pineapple slices instead.

The sequel to this came when we packed up to return to Juba three days later. Checking the rear of the lorry I was assailed by a most revolting stench. Peering over the tail-board of the lorry, I saw that the source of this was the remains of the fish given to us earlier.

"Dawedi!" I yelled for the obvious culprit.

Dawedi scuffed up in his usual manner.

"Sir," he said, with a broad grin on his face.

I pointed to the rotting fish. "What the hell's that doing on the lorry?"

"It is fish - for me - for Juba." explained Dawedi, with an unperturbed air as if taking a bunch of sweet-smelling flowers instead of a potential cause of an outbreak of food poisoning.

"If you want that fish." I told him "Then you can walk back to Juba with it. It's not coming on this lorry. Give it away - or throw it away."

We glared at each other for a few moments, then Dawedi removed the offending mass from the lorry and carried it over to the old hut he had used as a kitchen, where he draped it over the roof. He came back to the lorry and, as we moved away, he gazed despondently to where several Mandari were arguing over the remains of the fish, either being very hungry or having a poor sense of smell.

Five miles from Mongalla, on our way to the first village to be examined, we saw a number of vultures circling over the shrub, not far from the road. I stopped the lorry and asked the others if they had any idea of the cause of this. No one seemed to know so, rather foolishly, I decided to investigate. As we neared the vultures, a gazelle broke cover and bounded away into the cover of tall grass. The vultures rose heavily from the ground at our intrusion, then settled on the ground some distance away. The centre of their attraction was the remains of a gazelle, possibly the mate or mother of the one which had made off at our approach. The gazelle had been killed by hunters who had left the skin, head and bones. The eye sockets had been cleaned out by the vultures. After we left the scene the vultures returned, once more, to squabble over the remains. Ever watchful when circling overhead, they could be seen in large numbers over the slaughter ground at Juba on 'killing' days. Yet, in spite of their rather gruesome ways of feeding and far from handsome appearance, they were tolerated in some villages. At one they were to be seen walking through the huts like domestic fowl. Unperturbed, small children walked among them, safe, while alive but accepting the birds as part of the general scene. But while they did not suffer any great interference from people, they were attacked by hawks who took advantage of the vulture's inability to take evasive action at the moment of take-off. Then, as the slow, ponderous effort of the vulture to get into the air rendered it defenceless, the hawk hammered away at the vulture's unguarded head. But every vulture had its day, as was confirmed when, at the same village, one vulture was to be seen leisurely scraping flesh from a skin pegged out in the sun.

On the outskirts of the first village we were greeted by four young Mandari girls. At first they were inclined to be shy, but upon being shown their reflections in a wing-mirror, they forgot their shyness and pulled faces, roaring with laughter at their self-contorted features. One of the girls was of striking appearance. Her hair was thickly daubed with red clay (ochre?) and the same mixture smeared over parts of her body and face. Through one of her nostrils a ring of light-coloured metal was inserted and she wore ear-rings of metal, beaten out in a simple design. Around her neck and reaching below the level of her well-developed breasts were closely packed strings of brightly coloured beads. Circling her waist from ribs to legs, was a broad leather band, attached to which were numerous lengths of small-link chains, hiding the upper part of her thighs. On her wrists she wore heavy metal bangles, while around her upper arms were tight spirals of brass. A thin piece of buckskin was tied beneath each knee and this, in turn, connected with other pieces of buckskin around her ankles. Some of the Mandari girls we saw later wore, in addition to the above, heavy metal anklets, weighing several pounds.

Older women wore one or more strings of beads and a few coloured their hair. The main difference in costume between the older women and the girls was that the former wore a piece of cloth, or leather, from their waist almost to their knees at the front, together with a long trailing piece of leather covering their

23. Andrea examining women and children in Mongala

24. Gourd carriers

25. Women and girls Mongala

26. Women and girls

27. Old women

28. Old men

29. Assembling roof of grain store

30. Bodies of grain store

31. Complete grain store

32. 'Sausage' tree

33. Man on right carries 'Sausage'

34. Playing 'Holes in Ground' game

35. Long pipe

36. Scene near Lui

37. Patients out-station

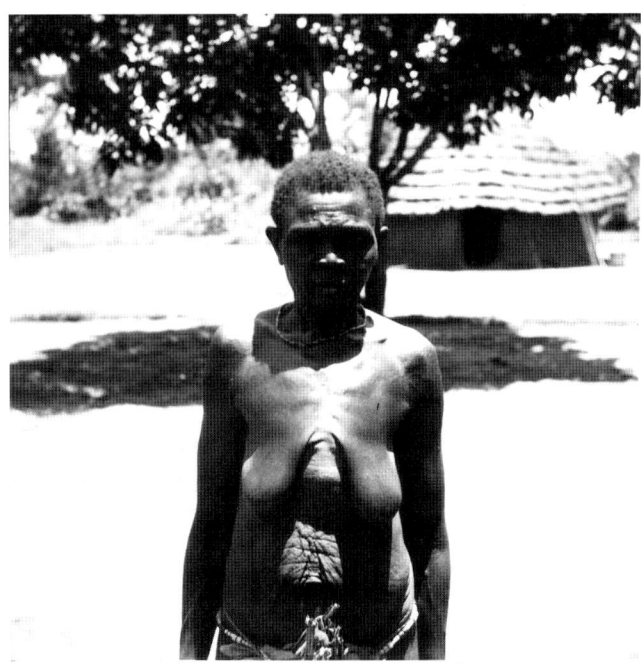

38. Old patient out-station

39. Grain delivery out-station

40. Woman kneeling in front of Elase - Lepromatous case

41. Goats on ant-hill

42. Mushroom ant-hill

43. Dokolo's

44. The Hunters

45. Bee-hive

46. Boys on guard

posteriors, instead of chains.

Pregnant women, having given birth, would suckle a child for up to two years and this resulted in a single distended breast or, in extreme cases, the distension was such as to allow the mother to feed a baby by pushing the breast back under her arm.

The older Mandari men wore little more than a necklace or two around their neck, but the younger men were flamboyant in their dress. A large feather was worn on the head, secured by a cord or a strip of cloth. Strings of coloured beads encircled their body, from the upper part of the chest to the hips, in the form of a corset. These strings were, in turn, secured at the back by long white beads stretching down the spine. In addition to this, bracelets of bound metal rings were worn on arms and legs while, attached to a necklace were decorative, polished metal discs hanging at the throat. They bore business-looking spears which laid to rest my thoughts of any effeminacy. The hard fibrous pods of the sausage tree were carried and these, up to two feet in length, were used as low ground seats. One might ponder as to whether the primary or secondary use of these was to prevent the procreative parts from dangling in the dust. But I didn't like to ask.

The photograph shows a group seated on the ground playing the "Holes in the Ground Game" (my definition). It has been described as a mixture of draughts, halma and solitaire*, needing a certain degree of numerical skill, even though the players had received no traditional lessons. The 'board' consisted of small holes scooped out in the ground and arranged in four rows, each row consisting of a dozen or more holes. In these were placed the

---

* Richard Wyndham – 'The Gentle Savage" (Cassell and Co. 1936)

'pieces' - usually ground-nuts. The first player to collect all the pieces was the winner. Usually a game lasted but a few minutes.

The game, thought to be Arabic in origin (although some have attributed it to other countries such as Greece), is played by both adults and children. Most villages had a board marked out in the shade of a tree.

The Mandari creative sense was demonstrated in their craftsmanship involved in the building of grain-stores, where their skills at wicker-work and thatching came to the fore. The completed store was placed on a raised platform and the roof, which was not attached to the body, was raised or lowered by means of a pole when grain was required.

As usual, local or passing natives came to us for treatment to cuts and minor abrasions. One man complained of a sore toe. The top had been sliced off by an acquaintance who, intending to stick his spear in the ground - had missed. One young lad brought to us by his father had a large open sore under his arm. Apart from cleaning up the area and covering it we could do nothing else. When I suggested to the father that he and his son come back to Juba with us so that the wound could be more effectively treated, he expressed reluctance to do so. This was understandable as Juba was about fifty miles away. He was persuaded, eventually, and came back to Juba with us. I gave him a couple of piastres for food.

Chapter 16

During the period when I was in the doldrums with regard to lack of transport and with little chance in the foreseeable future of the situation changing, two acquaintances asked if I would like to go hunting with them. I was not slow in taking up their offer. Ray was working on tsetse-fly control for the Sudan Veterinary Department, while John was on contract work in Juba, putting together an experimental grain-drying plant. We drove thirty miles south of Juba on the Nimule road. There were plenty of animal tracks at the sides of the road, but no sightings of any animals who could have made them. One of the locals we met on the road told us of a river-bed where game were to be found. Finding the location we parked the lorry by the side of the road, leaving Ray's driver with it. We then set off along the dry river-bed, my companions carrying their guns, myself a camera. The reflected heat from the sand and rocks underfoot was terrific, giving an indication of what to expect should you be tempted to sample the art of fire walking. Tracks of buck and buffalo criss-crossed the sand, sometimes finishing at small crevices in the rocks, which held unsubstantial amounts of scum-covered water. After walking for a mile or so in this unpleasant environment, we retraced our steps. Back on the road, we sat in the shade of the lorry and had lunch.

On the return to Juba we made another unsuccessful excursion into the bush, then got to wondering whether we had left it too late to catch the ferry back to Juba. But this was decided when a fault developed in the lorry and we had to stop until it was repaired. On arrival at the river we found the boat had gone over to the Juba side. We shouted across to the crew, who shouted back that they had finished for the day.

We sat on the river-bank in the growing darkness. The light from the lorry's headlamps, shining out across the Nile attracted hippo, who surfaced and blew us vaporous raspberries from their protruding nostrils. Two natives appeared out of the night and Ray asked them if they had a boat in which to take us across the river. One of them had a canoe, but expressed a reluctance to make the trip in the dark, because of the hippo. I felt relieved at this refusal, for hippo dodging in the dark had not appealed to me one bit. After discussing the situation for a while we decided to spend the night in a small resthouse about three miles away on the Mongalla road. As we drove along our headlights picked out the small forms of dove-like birds, nestling in the corrugations of the road. As we drove over them there were ominous thuds from beneath the lorry when birds failed to make successful flights to safety. Stopping at a small village on the way, we managed to buy a dozen eggs for our supper.

The resthouse was brick-built with a single door at the near end. Two small unwired gaps served as windows. Immediately to the front of the resthouse the ground was covered by sprawling figures. These turned out to be prisoners from Juba, under the charge of a solitary sergeant of police. The men were working in the vicinity, cutting bamboo and collecting grass for thatching. Stacks of these two items lay awaiting removal.

Lighting a fire we cooked the eggs and used the last of our water to brew up some tea. The mosquitoes began biting, forcing us indoors to our bed, which consisted of bundles of dried grass, covered by a tarpaulin. We undressed - that is, we removed our shoes. Sleep was difficult because of the mosquitoes. Even a squirt of repellent failed to have any effect. We tried, as a last resort, to sleep under the tarpaulin but that only gave us the option of suffocation. So, alternatively joking and cursing, we slapped our anatomy and resigned ourselves to a sleepless night.

There was a sudden half-groan, half-scream from outside. Putting on our shoes, Ray and John grabbed their guns and we went outside to investigate. Ray was of the opinion that it might be a calf being taken by a lion. The sound of raised voices coming from the village nearby seemed to confirm this belief. Approaching the continuing sounds of disturbance, we were flabbergasted to find that those blood-curdling noises were being made by a deaf mute. Having quarrelled earlier that day with a fellow villager, he was seeking revenge by trying to burn down his fellow wrangler's hut. We left them to it.

There was a full moon and the air, after the stuffy confines of the resthouse, was pleasantly cool. Sleep did not appear to be an ideal proposition, so we walked down the road instead. The hubbub of the quarrel died away behind us, to be replaced by the sounds of the bush. Hushed noises, stealthy noises. A drubbing of hooves to our right as several animals, possibly buck, raced off. To the left, in the distance, the high-pitched trumpeting of elephants joined the evening chorus. A movement in the ditch at the side of the road and an unidentified shape soon disappeared from view in the dark shadows of the surroundings. The brightness of the moon showed up the tracks of various animals as they made their way to the river. Returning at last to the resthouse we managed to get a few hours of restless sleep.

Several days later I again went hunting with Ray and John. But this time we stayed on the west bank of the Nile, taking the Luri Rokwe road to the extreme boundary of the Game Reserve. We first unsuccessfully stalked a large buck but were unable to get within range for a telling shot. A passing native, at our suggestion that he help us in tracking down game, helped us to a position forty yards downwind from a group of buck. Both my companions fired and one of the buck remained there standing, while the others raced away. Until that moment I had been as enthusiastic as they, but when I heard the bullets thudding into the body of a once graceful animal and then watched it slowly stagger and fall to the ground, all enthusiasm for the kill died. The wounds inflicted were not immediately fatal and as the animal struggled weakly, each wheezing breath brought fresh blood seeping from its mouth. I felt ashamed and when it was finally despatched with a fifth shot, part of me seemed to die too. I resolved that I would not take life, unless it was an absolute necessity.

The boys skinned and partly carved the carcase before putting it in the lorry. The native who had helped us was quite happy to receive the entrails as his share. He clutched the blood-dripping trophy in one hand, his spear in the other. It was dark by the time the meat had been prepared, so the native guided us back to the road. Trotting along before us, in the headlights' illumination and with the entrails dancing at his side, he resembled something out of a sausage-maker's nightmare. Memory of the kill remained with me for the duration of the tour and later I confined my 'shots' to those taken with a camera.

Towards the end of February 1952, the long-delayed arrival of a two ton lorry for survey work solved my transport problems. But not for long, eight days to be precise, for after that time I was due to take over at Lui, while Jimmy Roscoe went on six months leave to England. The new vehicle's most welcome feature was a built-in frame, holding two eight gallon water tanks. These, together with a spare tank I had borrowed from John Hannah, assured us of a future supply of clean water. With the lorry came a permanent driver - Dogu, a local Bari.

The time left to us gave the opportunity to complete the examination of the Mandari on the east bank, up to and slightly north of Mongalla resthouse. Passing the latter the vegetation thinned out and tall trees, which had been a feature further south, now gave way to stunted palms, forlorn-looking in their isolation amongst the short shrubs in the sandy terrain. North of the resthouse was a medium-sized, mixed community, the men working on an area of cultivation where bananas, pineapples etc were grown. Not only in competition from the weather, but also from the various animals who paused there on their way to the river. There was a Muslim influence here, demonstrated by the women, fully gowned, who refused to be examined. Fortunately for us the local medical assistant was able to persuade them, but only with the promise that no man would be present. It was a rather perfunctory examination up to the elbows and knees, plus the face, and really served no satisfactory purpose.

On the way back to Juba we examined several small villages which we had missed on our previous visit because of lack of time. Mid-afternoon we pulled in at one of the larger villages, just off the main road and where I intended to stay the night. As only a preliminary examination was possible that evening before dark, the rest of the people would have to be seen the following morning.

That evening after a meal I sat at my small table, enjoying a last cigarette before going to bed. The sky was clear, the air cool after the heat of the day and the brightness of the moon competed with that of the numerous stars. The atmosphere was peaceful, apart from vague noises emanating from the nearby village, together with the soft voices of the boys and a few villagers, seated around the dying embers of a fire. Suddenly, the stillness was shattered by the harsh foreign note of a car-horn. As its discordance approached, the vehicle's headlights could be seen, jumping this way then that, controlled by the vagaries of the road's uneven surface. I looked along the open space of ground towards the road and caught a quick glimpse of the culprit car and several of its occupants. Then it was gone and noise and illumination receded into the distance. I wondered upon the reason for all this disturbance. The next day I met the people concerned and they told me it was to scare away any animals. It hadn't exactly scared me but I must confess that in bed that evening I did consider whether or not lions hunted at night.

After completing our business the next morning and while packing up, I discovered that one of the supporting metal struts to hold a mosquito-net over a canvas camp-bed, which I had loaned to Andrea, was missing. Andrea had noticed it was missing the previous night but had not thought to tell me then as I was in bed. I mentioned the loss to the sub-chief and he said he would try and trace it for me. He did not appear to be unduly perturbed and eventually put forward the suggestion that one of the village boys had most probably taken it - to make a spear! I was not happy with this glib explanation and could not help venting my anger at the loss against him. He, in turn, insisted that his people were not in the habit of stealing from their own kin or from strangers, except, maybe if it were a lapse by irresponsible children. We did not part on the best of terms. Hours later I regretted my pigheadedness.

Later experience confirmed that the bush native was usually honest and helpful. On one occasion a native policeman cycled ten miles to return a notebook which had dropped out of the lorry, he having seen it fall as we were passing him. But, in a mixed community like Juba, circumstances created thieves. The cost of living being much higher than in the bush, the newcomer is tempted into stealing for goods he would like to have. In the bush he could quite possibly have bartered for his needs, but, in the town, he finds unsympathetic shopkeepers prefer piastres to peanuts. So he turns to thieving. One thief filched a blanket from my camp-bed which was outside the resthouse at Juba, in a rather conspicuous position. He tucked in the mosquito net after he had done so, which rather suggested a familiarity with European ways. A local policeman who investigated the theft went through what was obviously a set procedure when he measured the footprints in the dusty surroundings of the bed with a piece of straw, broken off until it was the right length. I don't know whether he compared the result with the footprints of the boy who had made the bed. Anyhow there was a negative result. This loss and that of the bed-rod, coming within a week of each other, made me security conscious for weeks afterwards.

At the last village to be visited before Juba, I was surprised to see the vehicle which had passed our camp the previous night. As we drew nearer I made out the figures of several Europeans, mixed in with a crowd of local villagers, on an open patch of ground near the village. I wondered what they were doing there and hoped their presence would not interfere unduly with my work, for I was hoping to get back to Juba by evening. Reaching the group, I saw that the natives were being carefully posed for photographs. The party consisted of a Belgian, in charge of the group, a Frenchman who was occupied with taking photographs of his wife, looking hopelessly out of place, wearing a floppy sun-hat and stylish dress, intent upon displaying her charms and splashing scent over nearby natives. The remaining member of the party was an English woman from Nairobi. They explained that they were making a film of bird-life in the area and that later that day they were moving north to a small lake where, so they had been told, they would find plenty of birds to satisfy their requirements.

Their camp was a short distance away and from where we stood I could make out a marquee and tents. I mentioned having heard and seen their passing the previous night.

They said they had seen my camp and asked why I had not dropped by to see them that evening when they had had a rather elaborate meal with iced champagne. I sighed inwardly as I thought of my own repast of tinned beans. They then enquired for the reason of my being in the area. I told them 'leprosy survey work'.

"Is there leprosy here then?" they asked, rather startled.

I thought of the comparison of their previous evening's meal with my tin of beans. So I just answered with a brief "Yes".

They had a brief discussion among themselves and then left abruptly, leaving me to get on with the survey without interruption or hindrance. Now they would have something else to talk about when they showed their photographs of scent-sprinkled natives later.

The only bribe I used myself was to take a photograph of one of the types of pipe in common use. This was when I placed the recipient of my tobacco in front of the rest of his group, thereby getting them all for one donation. Some of the pipes were ridiculously long, so much so that the owner had to get someone to light it for him. The usual method of lighting a pipe was to place a glowing ember on top of the tobacco in the bowl of the pipe. Usually the stem of a native pipe was of hollowed out bamboo, sometimes reinforced at intervals with metal rings. The bowl of the pipe was shaped from clay with a design carved or etched into the surface before it was hardened. Sometimes a piece of coloured cord or string would be attached to the bowl as a safety measure, in case it became loose on the stem. Pipes were smoked as much by women as men and it was not uncommon to see girls of fourteen years of age puffing away at their stubby 'clays' with obvious enjoyment.

Every village had its dogs. The native dog was smooth-haired, light-brown in colour, with white on the belly and feet. Most dogs had the appearance of being half-starved, as they ambled about with a lack-lustre air. When lying down, panting heavily in the heat, their skin rippled over prominent ribs, like the effect of wind on the surface of a field of grain. Water being at a premium, I never saw it put down for their benefit. Should a container of water be carelessly left on the ground they would seize the opportunity to drink it as fast as they could, with great slobbering gulps. Or, alternatively, as did the chickens, they picked up any human spittle spat onto the ground. The Bari and Lokoya tribes had little affection for their dogs, sometimes beating them unmercifully. In contrast, the Mandari usually controlled their animals with voice or threatening gestures. Whatever their use, the dogs were not given the status of pets.

On our return journey to Juba we were stopped on the road by a man in a high state of agitation. He told us that a truck had knocked down his cow and injured it so badly that he had had to kill it. The driver had not stopped. Unable to get the carcase to market he would lose financially. I remembered having seen a vehicle in the Mongalla area with a damaged radiator, so suggested to the man that he report the incident to the authorities. We offered him a lift to Juba, which he accepted. At the ferry we discovered that all vehicles and their registration numbers were recorded by a policeman who was on duty on the ferry for this purpose. So it appeared that the driver of the lorry would be identified.

Back at the resthouse in Juba I wrote up the results of our latest survey. The last for several months. Glancing at the pages of the booking-in book, I looked to see who had been there since my last stay. I then studied the column headed 'Complaints'. Some complaints were so lengthy that they filled the whole column from top to bottom. Others were more cryptic.

'Stove needs cleaning,'

'No sand in lavatory'

'Gaffir lazy and insolent - sack him!'

Sometimes there was an attempt at humour such as the old chestnut: 'The condition of the light switches is shocking.'

A Scot I met at Lameiga had expressed his concurrence with previous complaints by putting arrows from them to his contribution, written in a bold hand 'WHAT ABOUT SOME ACTION!'

Chapter 17 (Part 1)

I was not particularly enthusiastic about returning to Lui; the timing was far from propitious. There were several weeks of fine weather ahead during which time useful survey work could have been done. However, return I must, to enable the Roscoes to go on leave. For a week or so there seemed to be nothing but comings and going at Lui. Firstly, I arrived and took temporary lodgings in Dr Jim West's house, until the Roscoes left and I then changed houses. Not long after Dr West arrived, but his was a short stay, during which time he married one of the CMS sisters and they left the district to work in the Northern Nuer area. Apart from myself, the remaining European population consisted of two CMS sisters, Joan Bradford and Doris Handy, with Norah Holt, the schoolmistress of a mission school on the edge of Lui.

One morning I had occasion to call upon the sisters and was surprised to be introduced to an addition to our local society - Arthur Laxton, a replacement for Dr West. Slightly built and of rather boyish appearance, he'd looked too young to be a fully fledged doctor. A further surprise was when I found out later that he was a fellow Bristolian, although his accent did not give him away, as did mine.

During the brief interval between Dr West's leaving and Dr Laxton's arrival the house had been Gammaxined. This was common practice once a year and, because of the upheaval this procedure entailed, it would be quite fair to say that once a year was quite enough. The workers who did the job were well-known for the thoroughness in which they sprayed on the Gammaxine. Unfortunately this procedure, while much to the satisfaction of the operators, was not done with the selectivity that householders would have liked. Their motto would appear to have been 'If it moves - kill it. If it doesn't move - spray it.' Cognisant of this the householder made sure that all furniture was taken out of the building before the spraying began and before Sanitary Department employees were allowed into the premises to practise their often over-zealous exercise. Walls and ceilings were sprayed in what could only be described as an in-depth approach, due to the thorough drenching by Gammaxine. Such a disheartening prospect facing the householder for several days was offset to a certain extent by its being a necessary procedure to ensure freedom from the various pests. Proof of the spraying's efficacy could be seen within a short time by the corpses of scorpions and various insects strewn upon the floor.

The Roscoes' garden was fairly well established and, as they wished it to remain that way, I was obliged to take over their gardener. In addition, to make sure the house was kept up to scratch, I also included on my pay-roll the Roscoes' house-boy, Elisapa, who could also ensure that Dawedi's presence in the kitchen had no detrimental effect. There were also instructions regarding the few chickens and their eggs and the Rhode Island Red rooster. The garden, which abutted the main road was bordered by a high hedge, the thickness of which lessened daily, at one corner, due to the practice of young girls, on their way to the Mission school, picking new fore and aft coverings each day.

I brought back several packets of seeds with me from Juba, in the hope that I might grow my own cabbage, lettuce, carrots and beans, for these vegetables were virtually unobtainable outside of

Juba. I found some old boxes into which I put carefully sifted soil and planted the seeds. It was phenomenal the way they grew a matter of inches within a week. Having remained at this height for another week, they relinquished all attempt at future development and, finally, life. The lettuce and carrots did not put in an appearance at all, while the onions, after gracing the face of the soil with a downy-green, also succumbed to what I diagnosed as heat exhaustion. After this disappointing start I gave the remainder of the seeds to the gardener. This was a rather embarrassing moment for I had previously impressed upon him that I, and I alone, would be responsible for their growth. I was not entirely happy with the grin he gave at my surrender.

For a brief moment I harboured the suspicion that the seeds' demise had been aided by the gardener, who might have considered my doing his job an affront to his professional dignity. I was forced to accept his capability when, after giving him some beans to grow, they not only grew prodigiously but I was obliged to give a large number away.

Fresh vegetables were always a problem and except for the infrequent occasion when people passing through shared some of theirs, most of my vegetables came out of tins. There was a small area of cultivation on the banks of the River Yei, about five miles from Lui. I never got round to visiting it but was given to understand it was a small additional source of food for the colony and the hospital, cultivated by workers from both. The project was not a financial success because of the poor soil and, to some extent, by the lack of interest of the local people to buy any considered surplus. It was not that they disliked what was grown but rather that they did not accede to the idea of paying for it, rather they expected it to be given to them free of payment.

The question of over-cultivation of land was a very real problem at Lui, for the land there had been well-used for over thirty years and more. In 1952, the Agricultural Department, after an inspection of the soil, ordered that the land must be rested for not less than five years. There was no suggestion of a compromise, just an example of officialdom applying the rules with no consideration as to the consequences to the local community. It was said that a report would be sent but it had not arrived before I left. There was no constant supply of meat for the patients as funds would not allow it. A bull was killed twice yearly and a hippopotamus was killed every Christmas by the Game Department. Patients had little or no money to buy local meat, but some men hunted the long-tailed bush-rat.

Europeans had their meat problems but nowhere near the extent of the native, as the former had access to tinned meats, when needed. Tins were labelled with a picture of whatever they contained, whether meat, fish or vegetable etc., so that natives came to recognise what the tins contained. It was rather unfortunate that a worker for Save the Children had tins of baby food with an illustration of a baby on them. It was naturally assumed that the tins contained processed babies. The rumour grew. Could the weighing of their babies, said to be a check upon their well-being, be a ploy for choosing the best babies for the same purpose? Worried and confused, the mothers came up with an idea to thwart the white woman's gastronomic preference. While she was asleep they stole her false teeth from the bedside container. If this story is true - and it is plausible enough, then one must sympathise with the Save the Children worker, and hope that she had tins of soup in her stores.

Meat was sometimes available at Mundri, but as the animals were driven for several days prior to slaughter, the meat was not always in prime condition. It was an excuse to go there and visit Freda and Stanley May and their young daughter, Susan. Stanley was Vice-principal of the Teacher Training College there. In addition to the pleasure of their company, it was relief at times to get away from Lui for a while, especially when problems had piled up. Other Europeans at Mundri were Basil Chaplin, his wife and children and Ken Powell, a Tutor. Basil was Principal of the college and, prior to meeting him for the first time, I was under the impression that his Christian name was Charlie, having heard him referred to as such. On our first meeting I unwittingly addressed him as Charlie and wondered why he gave me a funny look, which included a slight tightening of the lips. I commented upon this to the Mays and they had a laugh at my slightly embarrassed expense.

A character I first met at Mundri, and whom I was to meet upon several occasions later in Juba, was Cliff Turner. He went under the imposing title of Inspector of Handicrafts for Equatorial Province. It suited him as he was a rather off-beat character himself, with an out-going attitude which tended to confirm the artistic temperament. His individualistic ways were at variance with those expected by his departmental superiors, such as his turning up at social gatherings clad in an orange coloured shirt, bright green gabardine slacks and sandals, instead of the usual simple dress of black trousers, white open-necked shirts, cummerbund, shoes or mosquito boots. Once he was reprimanded over the length of his hair, which was long enough to deflect the sun from the back of his neck - a natural adjunct against sunstroke which was not seen in that connection by authority which requested that Cliff get it cut 'for the reputation of the Department' forthwith. Cliff bowed to this request and came back from the barber's near-bald and looking like a monk whose tonsure cut had gone wrong. Needless to say his hair, or lack of it, was not mentioned again.

When based at Juba the problem of a haircut did not arise as there was always a barber to hand. At Lui the only chance of a haircut was when I went on the monthly visit to Meredi. Here was the Arab merchant who supplied the colony with cassava and grain on a casual basis, together with such household necessities as had been forgotten to order from Juba. He used several types of clippers which, while not as sharp as they might be, had a more reasonable effect and in a more conducive atmosphere, than that experienced with the barber at Pemba. He served up a rather peculiar brand of coffee, rather heavily spiced and which, to my unaccustomed palate, was like drinking a well-seasoned pork sausage. I usually tactfully refused a second cup. Of all the merchants I found him the most likeable and even though we had to converse through an interpreter, there seemed to be a certain rapport between us. Often he gave me fruit to take to Lui as a gift. I don't think this was just a sales gimmick, but I have no doubt it worked to his advantage. While Arab by birth, the old merchant was accustomed to southern ways, having lived in Meredi and district for nearly forty years.

Dawedi seemed to have settled down well in what would have

been to him a luxurious kitchen. His Saturday speciality was a mixed grill. I did not tempt providence by asking for more elaborate dishes. I had experienced a rather disastrous result of trying a variation of my usual breakfast of scrambled eggs. Dawedi's most redeeming physical feature was his infectious grin, which tended to soften any criticism of his work or activities. His awkward walk, coupled with a natural tendency to clumsiness made him somewhat of a menace waiting at the table. Generally, he suited my requirements and was reasonably successful in plain cooking requiring simple preparation. It was with this in mind that I decided to have a variation of scrambled eggs for breakfast by having my eggs boiled. Not only would this be a welcome change for me but, although I had not considered it at the time, it would also give Dawedi an extra string to his culinary bow.

"Dawedi," I said to him at an appropriate moment. "I'll have boiled eggs for breakfast."

He first assumed his thoughtful position with one hand cupping the opposite elbow, while he stroked his face with the fingers of the other. Seeing him in this posture I diagnosed his problem to be one of three things.

> 1. He wanted something he was unable to describe in English.
> 2. He was thinking of an excuse to get wages in advance.
> 3. Or, as in this instance, he was nonplussed.

At last, he shrugged his shoulders and confessed, "I no understand."

Leading the way to the kitchen I put the eggs in a pan of water and told him to bring the water to the boil and leave the eggs there for ten minutes. I gave him a clock and showed him the position where the hands would be when the eggs were done, at which time they should be removed from the pan. Dawedi seemed to have grasped this so I left him to it and returned to the house, where I became engrossed in a book. Twenty minutes later I realised, with a start, that the eggs had not arrived. At my shout of enquiry, Dawedi appeared.

"Eggs on fire." he confirmed to my repeated question as to where the eggs were.

"What!" I shouted and raced to the kitchen where I found two rather over-done eggs crackling and rolling about in a waterless pan from which heat-waves, rather than steam, were rising.

Dawedi looked on with an air of puzzled innocence.

"Make me scrambled eggs." I told him, my initial anger tempered by my hunger.

Dawedi and I had only a vague idea of making bread. An attempt at baking my own was considered upon Dawedi coming to me one day with something he had found in the Roscoes' kitchen. "How use me?" he enquired. Hastily scanning the instructions, which seemed clear enough, I said, "I'll show you."

It was a packet of yeast.

It seemed straightforward enough as full instructions were on the side of the packet. I carried out the preliminary mixing, watched intently by Dawedi and the houseboy. Finishing the kneading of the dough I placed it on top of the wood stove to rise. When this had occurred it had to be re-kneaded and then, when it had risen again, consigned to the oven. I had to go away on business almost immediately so told Dawedi to wait for half an hour, knead the dough once more, then put it in the oven.

"Yes." said Dawedi and the onlooking houseboy nodded his head as if in confirmation.

That evening I asked Dawedi to bring in the bread. He greeted this directive with one of his beaming grins. The sight of the bread when it appeared was rather a shock. Dawedi's happy expression had deceived me. Dawedi must have thought that the original state of the dough after my first kneading of it had been the desired finished state. To be frank, it resembled something deposited as a body function by a large animal with a bit of a problem. I gingerly cut myself a small piece, tasted it and hastily extracted it from my mouth. Because it did not appear to be humanly edible, I thought I would make a present of it to the Roscoes' chickens the following day. They raced towards the pieces I threw to them and then, just as hastily retreated from my intended treat. They grouped at one end of their enclosure making what I could only surmise as harsh voicing of complaint. Not long after, they stopped laying eggs. The rooster had stuck his beak into a rather gooey piece and spent some time shaking his head before finally getting rid of it. He then joined the chickens. Not long after, he went missing. Now I am not saying that the loss of eggs and the disappearance of the rooster were the direct result of their introduction to the bread. It was just a coincidence, but one of which I had been warned by the Roscoes. Eggs fertilized by the Rhode Island Red rooster were much prized by the local natives who were not adverse to stealing them to hatch out a superior breed. The rooster was abducted so that it might perform its natural function with the local breed. I had a hard job explaining this to the Roscoes when they returned and, quite naturally, left out the episode of the bread-making.

Andrea, my assistant, had returned to Juba where he was appointed dresser-in-charge at the leprosy village of Luri Rokwe, until we resumed the survey. To help me at Lui I had two experienced assistants in Elase and Elisapa. The former, besides acting as laboratory assistant, also handled the workmen and his knowledge of the general function of the colony was invaluable. I did not wish to introduce new ideas into the working of the colony, but rather to maintain those arrangements already in place until Jimmy Roscoe's return. Tall, lanky and speaking English well, Elase had been educated at one of the mission schools, being first employed at Lui CMS Hospital, before transferring to Lui leprosy colony.

Elisapa supervised the injections and general medical treatments which, if necessary, would be referred to the doctor at the CMS hospital. Seven dressers were under his jurisdiction, with both he and they being patients at the colony. Elisapa had been a medical assistant at Juba hospital until he had been diagnosed as having leprosy, when he was transferred to Lui for treatment, so he was fully capable of carrying out his duties. At times he was inclined to be surly, due to the drugs he was taking but also, to a great extent, to his realisation that his once promising medical career was, to all intents and purpose, finished.

General repair work in the colony had to be completed during the dry season. One of the worst chores was that of finding suitable sites for latrines because of the underlying rocky strata which, in most areas, lay but a few feet from the surface. To encounter this obstruction at an early stage of digging was far better than finding rock after digging down ten feet, when the regulation minimum depth had to be fifteen feet. The size of a latrine and its siting was dependent upon the number of people it was to serve - essential criteria in places such as Lui.

I had, rightly or wrongly, assumed from a conversation with Jimmy Roscoe before he left, that taking over at Lui should be a restful period, in comparison with the physical stress of survey work. As things turned out, I was exchanging physical for mental stress for it was rather unfortunate that my spell at Lui coincided with a grain shortage in the Moru area. Not only that. When grain was obtainable for distribution, particularly to the outstations, petrol was in short supply, so that priority had to be given to finding sources of grain and cassava flour. Sometimes, when this was done, word could be sent to the local chiefs explaining the situation and asking them to supply the substation in their area. They were usually co-operative for they knew that their costs would be covered.

The main problem lay closer to home - the colony itself. It was not feasible to send patients home until conditions improved, as this would interfere with their programme of treatment. There seemed to be only one solution and that was to cut the patients' rations until such time as the situation was rectified. In the meantime, the task of scouring the district for grain and cassava flour continued. It was a thankless task as demonstrated by the journey we made to Meredi - a round trip of one hundred and sixty miles - only to obtain two sacks of cassava flour. The immediate consequence of reducing the rations was that the majority showed their displeasure by going 'on strike', saying they would not co-operate; this, even though the situation had been fully explained to them, with the promise that things would return to normal when sufficient supplies were available There were still disagreements and eventually I was forced to impose rations upon them.

The situation went slightly in my favour after Elase reported to me one morning that several of the male patients had been found to be brewing beer. Not too serious a problem normally but as they were using grain rations to make the brew I was not, to put it politely, at all pleased. The containers with their fermenting beer were placed on the ground in a central area where they could be clearly seen. Having pointed out the error of their ways to the brewers, the beer was poured away in front of them and the mash burned.

As the position did not appear to be improving, I wrote to Juba explaining the situation and appealing for an urgent supply of grain if it was available. I had a reply saying that when grain was obtainable a supply would be sent. I heard nothing more for a week or so and then, a lorry arrived fully loaded with enough grain to see us through for the rest of the year. It might have been my reference to the supplies being needed also for the government substations which encouraged an early despatch.

Immediate attention was given to supplying the outstations. One of the most picturesque approaches to one of these was from Dokolo's, a village about seventy miles north-east of Lui. The leprosy outstation lay five miles further on. Dokolo's was named after the local chief, who might be said to be something of an extrovert. On a raised platform in the centre of the village were displayed a number of sun-bleached buffalo skulls, a public declaration of the chief's past hunting prowess. But this aspect of his life seemed to be over, for I did not see an increase in the number of skulls during the period of my visits.

Here, at the river Yei, where the water was calm and easy-flowing, was a sense of natural beauty that not only gave peace of mind, but also release from troubles, real or imagined, which had arisen at Lui. Gazing northwards, the view of the river might well have been that of a large English watercourse on a summer's day, with reflections of the clouds on the water and waterside trees standing at intervals like sentinels. But turning towards a bend in the river, the African aspect took over - a canoe being steadily propelled across the smooth surface of the river, head-laden women wading across the river through the shallows to the opposite bank, and, in the foreground, tribesmen gazed with lazy interest at the scene.

I moved to the edge of the river and was privileged to see what has been for me one of the sights of a lifetime. On a small patch of mud butterflies were resting, or slowly and alternately opening and closing their wings. But then, what took my full attention was a ballet of butterflies swirling in the air above them in a continual changing of pattern and colour. Truly a moment to be savoured by the senses. But the day was not yet over and I was to face another experience, of a different nature, which gave me an insight into a way of life adopted by some who had spent lonely lives overseas.

Not far from the village we had on several occasions become bogged down. This was usually encountered after rain when the sun had dried out the top surface, leaving a soft semi-mud layer below waiting for the unwary. Most times when this occurred someone had been available to help us out. On this particular occasion our helper was a young woman who came over to where I was struggling at the rear of the wagon, while Manoa was doing his thing in the driver's seat. She indicated she would help and went over to the side and bent over to push, at the same time displaying a neat pair of buttocks, barely covered by a bunch of leaves. The truck suddenly lurched forwards and we were both bespattered with mud from head to toe. For a few seconds we looked at each other before bursting into spontaneous laughter. At that moment she became a person and the barrier I had put between myself and those I had examined previously crumbled a little. With this came an understanding of why some Europeans had taken native women as mistresses or wives.

There but for the grace of God go I. Or maybe would or could have done if I had not subdued my inclinations.

An example of this is given by Richard Wyndham in his book 'The Gentle Savage' (Cassell - 1936). A government official, with whom he had spent two months within the Dinka tribal area, had married a Dinka girl and later they had a son. On retirement, the official remained in the area with his family until his death. After reading the book, which I had obtained from the CMS bookshop at Juba, I enquired as to what had happened to the official's wife and his son. I was told that she had become Matron of a school (Mission?) and her son had received a good education.

Not long after my return to Lui, a young woman with a child presented herself at the colony. Elase explained that she had been sent from Lui by Jimmy Roscoe some months before, when she was found to be pregnant. I spoke to the woman who told me that a teacher/patient in the colony was the father of her child. These facts were confirmed by Elase. She went on to explain that she already regarded the teacher as her husband. When I asked her why she had taken it upon herself to return, now that Jimmy Roscoe was away, she replied that her parents had turned her out because of her illegitimate child. Uncertain, and not fully conversant with the original facts of the case, I made it a condition of her staying at Lui for the present that the father of the child agreed to marry her. This he agreed to do and so she was allowed to remain while the necessary arrangements were being made. I thought the problem on hold for the time being.

A week or so later I had complaints about the new arrival fighting with other women. Things finally came to a head one evening when the newcomer tried to set fire to the hut occupied by a woman with whom she had quarrelled earlier that day. What made the action more serious was that several young girls also lived in the hut. Sending for the woman I told her that she would have to leave the following day and would have to settle details of her marriage to the colony teacher with her chief. The night before she was due to leave she attempted suicide by swallowing a poisonous root. Arthur Laxton was called in time and by making her swallow copious draughts of salt water, he succeeded in getting her to vomit up what she had swallowed. I realised then how little I had understood the woman's problems, that she should have attempted to take her life. The following day, when she was fit to travel, we took her to Amadi as attempted suicides had to be reported to the D.C. When the case was heard a few days later the colony teacher was told that he would have to accept the normal responsibilities of being a father, within his limited means. But what seemed to be important was that marriage would confirm the legitimacy of the child. I never learned of the result before I left.

On one occasion when Manoa, the colony driver, and I went to Meredi it began to rain so heavily that the roads became flooded. Rather than attempt to travel the eighty miles back to Lui in the dark, we stayed at the Bishop's house. For those stranded, as we were, it was an open house. Should the Bishop be away, the only obligation being that you paid the servant for his services. After an evening meal I sat in the main room to browse through a book I had taken from one of the several book shelves there. The rain was particularly heavy, with a background of thunder and lightning. From where I sat I noticed a dark scorch-mark on the opposite wall. It gradually dawned on me that it had been caused by lightning and, turning my head, I saw a similar mark on the wall behind me, with myself directly in line between the two. Now, as lightning has been known to strike more than once in the same place, I moved out of the line of fire. But Nature behaved herself and there was no repetition of the previous incident that night.

Upon our return to Lui the following morning, Elase came to the house with a tin of hashish and a pipe for smoking it. He had taken them from one of the patients the previous day in my absence. I was obliged by law to report the find so had to bring it to the attention of the D.C. at Amadi. The patient concerned was bound over but warned that any future use of the drug would make him liable to imprisonment. This more of a knuckle-rapping threat than a possibility, for the patient's condition would have made his detainment in a civil jail unlikely. I talked with the D.C. and emphasised that my concern was the fact that the patient had been supplied from outside sources, and that the people concerned should be the ones to be punished. He was quite in agreement with my sentiments and commented that he had sympathy for the patient whose active life had been curtailed by leprosy. Not long afterwards I was told that two men, who lived near the colony, had been responsible for supplying the drug. They had been found guilty of receiving and supplying and sent to prison for several years.

It had been estimated that some 25% of the local population smoked hashish and this included some of the colony patients. I had been blissfully unaware of this situation until the above circumstance. It seemed certain that infiltration of the drug was inevitable.

Chapter 17 (Part 2)

A note from one of the CMS sisters, Joan Bradford, told me that there were two men fighting in her compound, one of whom was a colony patient. Would I come down right away. I went immediately and she showed me one of the nearby huts from which sounds of a struggle were coming. I tried the door but found it jammed. Considering it might be unwise to enter the hut because of this difficulty, plus the fact that I would have to enter in a crouching position due to the low doorway, I stood back and kicked the door open and shouted at the two struggling figures on the floor. They came out and I grabbed one whom I recognised as the man from the colony. He had a nasty looking gash on his forehead. I took the patient to the colony and sent word to Arthur Laxton to come over and stitch the wound, which was bleeding profusely. When Arthur arrived, I held the man while he inserted the necessary stitches. I had to hold the man's head firmly while this was being done, with the result that my shirt was saturated with blood. Not wanting the patient's blood next to my skin, I hurried back to the house, washed and changed. I threw out the shirt as a potential hazard, for most leprosy is spread by close contact.

The other man involved in the scuffle made himself scarce while I was doing this and I later found out that he had caused trouble at Lui on previous occasions, once fighting with one of the colony teachers over the possession of an ant-hill. This might appear to be a trivial reason over which to quarrel, but it was a prized possession among the local natives and handed down from one person to another. The mature ants were eaten as a delicacy. Some Europeans had been known to fancy them.

At certain times of the year, dependent upon the weather conditions, future Kings and Queens left the nest to take part in a wedding flight. At night, or in the early hours of the morning, hundreds of ants would leave the nest and fly; many did not last long enough to consummate their destiny because man, not their natural predators - birds and lizards, awaited them with lighted torches of twisted grass to singe off their wings, after which they a dropped down into shallow depressions scooped out in the earth to receive them.

It was on such a night that the tragedy occurred.

One of the young patients at the colony was suffering from a form of oedema which was affecting his brain. I was not conversant with his past history until one day, upon returning from a visit to an outstation, I was confronted with the news that he had tried to hang himself from a tree on the outskirts of the colony. The attempt failed when the rope snapped and his unconscious body was discovered by two other boys. After this I put a dresser with him as a 'minder'. When he appeared to have recovered, I asked him if he would like to continue with his school lessons while he was in the sick ward. He agreed, so I told the school-teacher to supervise this in the hope that this would keep him occupied, but mainly that he should be kept under close observation. Unfortunately, some of the other boys treated his condition as a joke and taunted him and it was not possible to prevent this happening entirely. The lad began having illusions during which he insisted that someone was taking his money. On one occasion, whether or not he was egged on by other boys (some of whom, I suspected, were among the boys who had asked for a pay rise soon after the Roscoes' departure and which I had refused) he threatened to knock me on the head with a large stone - if I did not return his money. One day he almost succeeded and if Elase had not shouted out a warning as the lad was creeping up behind me, at the same time grabbing him, he might well have carried out his intention. After this I arranged with Elase to have a dresser with him night and day. This, to all intents and purposes, solved the problem. Until the night of the ants.

At midnight on that evening Elase woke me with the news that the lad had disappeared from the sick-bay.

"How did this happen?" I exclaimed with a sense of shock. "Wasn't the dresser with him?"

"No," replied Elase. "The dresser left him to collect his ants." I swore to myself. "Have you searched the grounds?"

Elase confirmed that this had been done, adding that the lad might have gone home. I told him to continue the search for a little longer and, if this were unsuccessful, then Manoa, the colony driver, and myself would visit nearby villages in the morning to verify whether or not anyone had seen him.

The following morning, at dawn, as there had been no sign of the lad, Manoa and I drove around the local villages, but without success. We drove back to the colony. On its approach road Arthur Laxton stopped us with news that the missing lad had been found.

"Good," I said with relief, "where is he now?"

Arthur swallowed and found difficulty in replying at first. "They've cut him down. He hung himself last night. On the big mango tree beyond the huts."

I could say nothing. Further away in the colony a group of girls were filling the air with their harrowing death wails. The body had been carried into the treatment room and lay on the table there. I stood there alone for a while looking down at the boy. His face bore an expression of peacefulness. A peace which was shattered for me as I watched a solitary ant crawl from a nostril.

It was now approaching mid-day so I gave word that the colony workmen should begin digging a grave, ready to inter the body the following morning. I contacted Pastor Anderea, the native pastor, and arranged the burial with him. The next morning, when the body had been placed in the grave, the pastor was surprised when I asked him to say a few words and it was with obvious reluctance that he eventually did so. For me, the fact that the lad had taken his own life bore no relationship to paying him our last respects. The unfortunate lad had been a victim of circumstances and compassion was needed, rather than rejection. No doubt the pastor offered up a prayer for himself for his part in the ceremony.

The boy's death, and the subsequent sight of the ant on his face as the body lay upon the table, was a sight I have never forgotten although, many years later, the passion I felt a that moment has gone. Later, at Juba, when relating this episode to Bishop Oliver Allison, my lips suddenly stiffened and I was unable to speak. My companion hurriedly looked away until I had recovered. I also found that from that time I became somewhat irritable. A week's leave in the coolness of the hills east of Liria would have helped but Jimmy's imminent return would not allow for this. So, for a while, I walked hand-in-hand with self-pity. A most hateful companion.

In spite of the set-backs I had experienced, some degree of balance was maintained by my interest in nature. There was no need to look far for the house itself provided a selection of creatures in various shapes and forms. The most common type of lizard was about seven inches long when fully grown. The back of the male was a brownish green with light yellow on its under-parts. But the male's most distinctive feature was the black, yellow and green spots intermingling with a rather bizarre effect, under the lower jaw and neck. The female had broad alternate stripes of light and dark green running down the length of her back, while the under-part was a pale yellow, as the male. However, her most distinctive feature was a tail of brilliant blue.

Another type of lizard was the Koggelmonetjie (the South African name meaning 'the little mimicking man'). This referred to its rather amusing habit of bobbing up and down to look around corners, or over obstacles. The male is of striking appearance, mainly black, with head and crest of bright turquoise and a golden coloured tail. The female is smaller and of a dull brown colour. One particular female of the species frequented the branches of a mulberry tree at the edge of the veranda, taking up position in a lower fork. From here she shot out her long tongue to pick off ants making their way down from the upper branches, where they had been 'milking' a species of greenfly. The lizard allowed the ants to walk upwards over her body unmolested but swallowing with great rapidity those coming back down.

Lizards were preyed upon by that sharp-eyed predator - the hawk. Standing close to a wall and preparing to photograph a lizard basking in the sun I was startled by the rush of wings as a hawk brushed against me and seized my subject. It flew up into a nearby tree and proceeded to devour it ravenously, now and then looking around to make sure it would not be interrupted.

At evening, the nocturnal geckos made their appearance on the mosquito-wired windows, waiting patiently until a fly, moth or other insect attracted by the light from the room, came within reach. The lizard's skin colouring of marbled brownish grey helped to hide it in the broken light and its ability to race quickly over the wire was made possible by special features of its toes' bulbous ends.

Inside the house at night insects constantly circled the oil-lamps. Some approached too close and died, except the one occasion when a small grasshopper leapt upon the glass, slithered off and then, to my astonishment, put its scorched feet in its mouth, very much as humans do with their fingers under a similar situation.

Walking on the veranda one day, I trod on a fair-sized, black beetle. Withdrawing my foot, I was surprised to find that the beetle was till intact and, within a short time it moved off, apparently without any distress. In comparison a furry caterpillar I picked up to examine more closely ejected its numerous bristly hairs and these caused considerable agitation for some time.

There was little game in the surrounding area, although from time to time buffalo and lion had been known to pass that way. I saw lion on two occasions. The first time it was dead, having been shot by game scouts after it had been prowling around the cattle enclosure one night. It showed signs of an old wound which, no doubt, had prevented it from hunting normally.

On the second occasion the lion was very much alive. Elase roused me one night to tell me that a lion had been prowling around the colony. There was nothing we could really do except warn the people nearby and especially those at the CMS hospital. We aroused Manoa and taking the pickup, drove down to the colony to warn the patients to secure their huts and stay indoors. The lights of the pick-up were not working properly so Elase stood at the side of the door and shone his torch ahead of us. From the colony we drove to the hospital to warn the patients who were sleeping outside on the veranda. After our initial warning they picked up their bedding and disappeared into the safety of the hospital interior. We were amused at the speed with which they disappeared.

As we drove back slowly to the house Elase spotted the lion on the large open space in front of the boys' school, eyes gleaming in the light of his torch. The colony carpentry instructor jumped to the ground and fitted an arrow to his bow, then let fly in the direction of the lion. The gleaming eyes disappeared - then showed once more. The arrow must have dropped near the lion and it had turned its head to see what it was. Another arrow was despatched and the lion made off into the darkness. There was nothing else we could do. The people had been warned, so we went back to bed. In the morning tracks were found near the boys' school, colony and hospital. A game scout was sent for and though he spent a considerable time looking around, and stayed that night at Lui, his vigil was unsuccessful, so it was assumed the lion had left the area.

Fortunately, the hills surrounding Lui were free from leopards, or at least none had been seen. But Mundri were less fortunate and during one period of three weeks three leopards were trapped and killed. The type of trap used was a wooden one, built on the surface of the ground. The side consisted of thick wooden stakes about six feet long, driven into the ground a few inches apart. The structure was some seven feet in length and eighteen inches wide and completely blocked at the top. At the closed end was a small compartment in which a goat was tethered as bait. As it was not possible to reach the goat from the outside the leopard was obliged to try its luck by entering the open end and, by so doing, released a spring which allowed a log to fall and prevent its escape.

Never a day went by without our seeing groups of baboon on or near the road when we were travelling. They were in all shapes and sizes, from large males to the very young being given a ride on their mother's back. While they would remain close to the road if you stayed in your vehicle, to step outside was potentially dangerous when a large male would face us and bark a warning to the rest of the group who would scatter in the trees. Manoa and I surprised a large female as she was crossing the road and, as she turned to face us when we stopped, we both burst out laughing to see she was carrying a large orange in her mouth, obviously stolen from a nearby village. Baboon are inveterate plunderers and can play havoc with crops.

At the peak of the dry season the house became the roaming ground of the Jerrymunglums, sometimes referred to as Camel spiders. They were not spiders, although they bore some resemblance to them. Their swiftness of movement had to be seen to be believed. One moment they would be peering at you over the edge of the table facing you, the next over the edge of the table to your left and then, in a flicker of movement, to your right. Once you had got over the initial shock of their antics they were fascinating to watch at their game of "Now you see us - now you don't".

Compared with this astonishing exhibition of movement were the more leisured perambulations of a striped mouse, who visited me for a short period each evening, usually as I sat reading a book. I would first become aware of its presence as it wandered over my feet, inspecting shoes and socks, until its persistence became too disturbing and I waved it away. One afternoon, in the throes of a siesta, I was disturbed by the sound of a mouse gnawing its way through a box containing some of the Roscoes' things which they had packed prior to going on leave - for safety. There was nothing for it but to investigate, with the help of Dawedi, carefully removing the contents until the culprit was discovered; a striped mouse which Dawedi caught, put on the floor and stamped upon with his big feet. I felt rather sorry at the mouse's demise in this way as I had become accustomed to its nightly visits. That evening I was reading a book, as usual, when there was a familiar nibbling at my feet and my loneliness ended. My companion was back.

On my last visit to Meredi, before returning to Juba, I was faced with several problems. The first concerned an accusation by one patient against another. The accused, an Azande, was charged with cannibalism. The accusation was not lacking in substance for facts proved, by no less an authority as Evans Pritchard, that cannibalism amongst the Azande had taken place in earlier days, although it seems to have been restricted initially to enemies killed in battle and people executed. But the latter only occasionally and to certain individuals.

But the situation needed to be resolved so I asked the dresser-in-charge to call the patients together, then count them. When this had been done I asked, loud enough for all the patients to hear, whether all were present.

"Yes." The dresser confirmed.

"Then, if everyone is here, no one has been eaten."

The accuser was still adamant that his accusation was correct. So I told him that if anyone had been eaten, it must have been someone outside the village and this did not concern me. I suggested that if he wished to pursue the matter further, he should contact the local D.C., who had jurisdiction over people outside the village.

The patients laughed when they heard this and poked fun at the accuser.

Because of the Azande tendency to promiscuity in past years, in 1945 and 1955 surveys showed that in a group of one hundred women, the number of children could be counted on the fingers of one hand. This was, on the whole, due to infertility caused by V.D. The Azande women, when I worked in the area, had a tendency to make obscene suggestions or sing lewd songs.

On one occasion when, having a lift to Meredi by the Lui Mission School teacher, we happened to stop near several Azande women. They looked into the cab, made a remark and then laughed. My companion, obviously embarrassed and angry, replied to whatever had been said. When I asked what had been said she refused to tell me. Now, I assume that it had sexual overtones.

No sooner had the Azande episode been dealt with than a patient with bandaged feet and hands complained that during the night mice nibbled at the bandages. Would it be possible to get a cat for him? At the time this appeared to be a simple enough request to fulfil, for the Mays' cat had recently given birth - courtesy of a feral tom which frequented the area. Freda, maybe a little lightheartedly, had asked me if I would like one. In a moment of bonhomie I tactlessly agreed to this with the proviso that the need was that of someone else. Little did I know then that this promise would lead to a situation of greater complexity than the complaint about cannibalism. I had not really thought the situation through and my impetuosity gave rise to several problems. The first was that I had forgotten I would not be visiting Meredi again before I returned to my survey work. The second, which confronted me upon my arrival back at Lui, was that the following day the Gammaxine men were due to arrive to have their way with the Roscoes' house - a visitation which had slipped my mind. Having collected a kitten from the Mays on my journey back from Meredi, I was obliged to let Elase have it to look after, for the time being, as I would be spending some time at Arthur Laxton's until the Roscoes' house was habitable again. I crossed my fingers, but this was a forlorn gesture as was proved by future events.

The kitten got away from Elase and later turned up at Arthur Laxton's house, where it sought refuge in the drain fronting the veranda and at the base of a small flight of steps. The drain acted as an echo-chamber for the kitten's howls of despair and, no doubt, hunger. Attempts to lure it out failed but one evening, after dark, as I sat in the living room, a pair of gleaming eyes appeared at the top of the steps. I moved and frightened the kitten away. The following evening I put a dish of bread and milk just outside the door and watched the kitten feed in the semi-darkness. The next evening I placed the bowl inside the room, partly under a chair. The kitten, after a sniff around, fell upon the food and growled its way through the meal. Several evenings later I was able to entice it upon my lap, where it purred softly and apparently contentedly. Suddenly the peace was shattered by the high pitched note of a trumpet. It was Arthur relieving himself of tension. The protracted note showed that the player had quite a bit of tension to dissipate. My immediate reaction had been to jump while the kitten sank its claws into my groin. I was wearing shorts at the time and the combined pain and shock was excruciating. This was followed by a quick lunge to the floor by the kitten and its disappearance out of the door. There was no further noise from the kitten that night. Quite possibly because Arthur continued playing for a while. I left not long afterwards and never did find out whether or not it was taken to the patient at Meredi.

I had a rather frantic letter from Jimmy Roscoe saying that he was delayed in Khartoum because of a misunderstanding about a reserved seat on the southbound 'plane'. Could I go to Juba to meet Dr Cochrane, the BELRA Medical Secretary, who was making a tour of the BELRA colonies in Africa.

When the arrival of Dr Cochrane was imminent, I set off to Juba. Some weeks before I had had occasion to visit the town in order to make myself known to the new hospital doctor, a Northerner, who had succeeded Dr Wheaton as Equatorial Province

Medical Officer. I was carrying with me a report for the Governor, from Basil Chaplin, Principal of Mundri Training College. This concerned the visit of Northern visitors to the college. Not being privy to Basil Chaplin's side of the story, I only knew what I had gleaned from others.

Apparently, when the visitors entered one of the classrooms, they were angered to find that the content of the lesson was based on the Arab slave-trade. The teacher responsible was something of an authority on this as his great grandfather had been taken by Arab slavers. The visitors seized the opportunity to imply that this confirmed their suspicion that anti-Northern propaganda was being imposed upon Southern students. This innuendo was false. If anything, it may have been a case of opportunism on the part of the teacher to express his and others' fears that the North was not to be trusted, even though elections were to be held.

The visitors themselves were not blameless in the matter of intimidation. On their way to Juba, by air, they had flown extremely low over at least one village, terrifying the people. I could well imagine the impact this had had on the villagers as once, as we drove into an isolated village, we were astonished to see the villagers leaving the village on the far side to take cover among some trees. I sent Andrea ahead to explain the reason for our calling there. They were eventually persuaded to return and they, mainly women and children, laughingly explained their reaction was due to the fact that it was the first time a lorry had entered their village.

After we had examined the people who were available, a small boy, standing by his mother, began to 'play up'. She bent and spoke softly to him and whatever she said brought an immediate grimace on her son's face, which turned to that of horror as he looked my way. He then disappeared quickly behind his mother, from where he gazed at me with tear-glinting, distrustful eyes. It's a small world, I thought, having heard the same threat being made to white children by their mothers, only in this instance a coloured person would be used as a threat.

When I had first met the new Medical Officer, we discussed the survey I was undertaking as he was not conversant with its purpose at that time. However, I was surprised and somewhat unimpressed with his attitude towards a member of staff who came to the office with a query. The lad was met with brusqueness and a rather intolerant attitude which, together, made him nervous and near incoherent. The doctor lost his temper and shouted at the lad to get out. Then, turning to me and possibly feeling obliged to explain the reason for this display, he said "These people! They don't speak Arabic - very little English. They're useless!"

It appeared obvious that he found his posting to Juba, to say the least, rather irksome in comparison with his former way of life and this contributed to his present state of mind. While one could, to some extent, sympathise with his predicament, it did nothing to endear him to the Southerners who were under his authority and with others with whom he came into contact. His lack of comprehension of the political situation which was developing was something he could well have done without, especially with the South's fear of unqualified subjugation when they would have a minor voice in government.

A small party of Dr Cochrane, the Medical Officer and myself first visited the largest government leprosy village in the area at Luri Rokwe, about seven miles north of Juba. Here we were joined by Andrea, who had taken charge of the village after we had completed the first part of the survey. From there we went to the small leprosy village in the Latula area, not far from Liria and where we had arranged to meet Chief Lolik Lado. Viewing the small groups of huts with their elderly occupants, some of whom were 'burnt-out cases', it was obvious that the conditions at the site left much to be desired. The two doctors sat alone, no doubt discussing what they had seen, while I stayed with Lolik Lado and Andrea. Tea was produced and I was offered some, but there was none for the chief and Andrea. Shortly, I went over to the chief and gave him a cigarette as a token of sympathy. Then, I was called back over to have lunch with the others, but ate little, tense and ashamed at the lack of courtesy shown to the chief.

I compared this situation with the light-hearted tea-break early in the survey. The chief and I sat upon chairs under a large mango tree, sharing some of the large fruit. In return, I offered the chief some tea from my flask. He accepted the offer with alacrity and sent someone off for a cup. When the man returned, the cup was enormous, capable of containing more tea than I could supply. My feeling of bewilderment must have showed in my face. I glanced at Lolik Lado and saw a twinkle in his eye. I commented that my offer had been for the chief only - not the whole tribe. He laughed when Andrea translated for him, as did the crowd of onlookers. Later that day he sent me over a guinea fowl he had shot.

Dr Cochrane then visited Lui for a few days, during which time he familiarised himself with the work of the colony. We had not reached Lui without incident for the lorry in which we were travelling broke down when we were half-way there. Fortunately, another lorry came along going in the same direction and the doctor and I were lucky to obtain a lift. The driver stayed with our original transport and said he could put it right. In fact, he turned up at Lui the following morning having made an inadequate repair to the exhaust, which needed replacing, so we had to send for a new unit.

Whilst in Lui Dr Cochrane stayed with Dr Laxton, as had been previously arranged so that they were able to talk shop with each other. He then returned to Juba before going on to complete his itinerary in other parts of Africa.

A few days later Jimmy Roscoe returned and I put him in the picture concerning things which had taken place in his absence. Sometimes he gave a grimace to show that he did not entirely agree with what I had done but I consoled myself with the fact that he had not been confronted by the situations at the time and which, very often, were controlled by my not trying to change the routine already established. I must confess that it was with a sense of relief that I left Lui and returned to Juba to commence the final stage of the survey.

Chapter 18

I arrived back in Juba to be confronted, once more, by a petrol shortage and there was little likelihood of my being allowed any to continue the survey. While enquiring in the A.D.C.'s office about the situation, the door was thrust open and a rather brash American entered. In his hand he brandished a piece of paper at the A.D.C with the remark, "Here's the paper to tear down the walls of Jericho". It was permission for him to obtain as much petrol as he needed. His team was involved in some American controlled international project, the essence of which I never discovered.

But the episode put my frustration up a few notches and I began to wonder whether the survey would ever be completed before my tour ended. One inconvenience of our lorry was that it only did eight miles to the gallon, which meant that we took a fair amount of petrol with us to cover the return journey from our forays out of town. For example, on a trip to the Mongalla area, we were obliged to carry fourteen four gallon tins of petrol. This not only to cover the journey there and back but also to take in villages not shown on the maps.

There was nothing to do but settle down at the resthouse in Juba until things became more normal. I had several long trips to make and was impatient to complete them. I had not been there long before I had a message from Colonel Mallory, whose house was nearby, asking me to call. I was puzzled as to why he wanted to see me. When I arrived at his house he was full of apologies and explained, in a rather worried tone, that he suspected one of his houseboys had leprosy. His fears were confirmed when I found several tuberculoid lesions on the man's body. An added complication was that he was married. With his permission and that of his wife, she was given a cursory examination of her arms and legs only. This was in respect of the fact of their being Muslims. There was, of course, the possibility that she may have given the disease to her husband, from the close contact of marriage.

There was also the problem of what Colonel Mallory should do with regard to his servant's future. When news of the man's affliction became known, there would be a falling off of visitors. I pointed out to Colonel Mallory that there was treatment available but there was still the dilemma of where the servant should live as it would not be acceptable that he now continued to work in the house. Could an outside job be found? The ball was in the Colonel's court and I never learnt which way it bounced.

Small quantities of fuel became available and we were mobile once more. We first made journeys of up to sixty miles or so along the Juba - Lui road. Bari, Fejula and Nyambura tribes had villages on or not far from the road. One outstanding feature when working in this area was the near nightly sound of drums, a throbbing rhythm which carried on the airwaves to intrude upon your awareness, to the exclusion of all else. At times your very pulse seemed to take on the drum's cadence. Very few dances finished before the early hours of the morning. Dancers and onlookers sang with the same repetitious note as the drums, the dull monotone of the men intermingling with the shrill high-pitched voices of the women.

Early one morning, after a sleepless night, I arrived at the village we were to examine that day and where they had held a dance the night before. I thought everyone would be exhausted after their all night activities. But - no, they were as chirpy as ever. One young lad of about three years of age danced about with unflagging gusto and quite possibly with skill, as he performed his steps. I remarked about this to the sub-chief.

"He should be good - he was up practising all night."

The sub-chief laughed "There is no dance tonight." he said "So you will be able to sleep."

I asked if the dance had been held for a special occasion and he replied that this was one of the usual Saturday dances.

Sitting in the schoolhouse which I had made my quarters, reading in the light of the oil-lamp, out of the corner of my eye I became aware of a movement at floor level. It was located in one of several holes near the outer wall. I looked towards it warily, hoping it was not a snake and contemplating what evasive action I would take if it was. A head appeared - followed by a squat body and revealed itself as a frog. Without delay it waddled to the base of the wall and eased itself into the thick accumulation of dust until only the head and eyes were visible. I was soon made aware of this ploy when the frog shot out its tongue now and again to retrieve bodies of moths or various insects which had fallen foul of the hot glass, or rising heat from the lamp.

Several days later I experienced the biggest scare I had during my travels. We were staying in the schoolhouse near another village, on the same road. Because of the humidity I was sleeping in the open on one side of the building, the boys on the other. It was a bright starry night with a moon. A small group of natives passed by, unseen in the darkness but their presence made known by their raised voices, used as a deterrent to warn off any animals in the vicinity. The boys were laughing and joking for a while and then, at last, when the talking had subsided, the hitherto subdued noises of the night made themselves heard. The odd mosquito and the dry rustle of the heads of dura on their eight foot stalks that bordered the edge of the open space some thirty feet from where I lay in bed. Closing my eyes I relaxed, before giving myself over to sleep. I was brought to wakefulness by a sound coming from the inside of the school. Half-raising myself on my elbow I listened carefully and now the sounds could be identified as the movement of tins. One of the boys helping himself to sugar? Keeping an eye on the doorway through which the culprit would have to emerge, I waited. But the figure, when it came, did so on four legs, not two. My God, I thought - a leopard. I'm about to be eaten when due to go home shortly. Without further ado I pulled the blanket over my head in an attempt at concealment. After a while, hearing nothing more, I peered cautiously out. The animal sat facing me from the edge of the dura and was staring in my direction. It was then I noticed large tufted ears and, with a certain relief, realised that my visitor was a lynx. It settled in a crouched position, probably wondering what the mosquito-netted bed was. I began to suspect it was tensing itself for a spring. Throwing all thought of composure to the wind I shouted for the boys. No answer. I shouted out individual names. Still no reply. But the last shout seemed to disturb the lynx and it loped off into the shadows. If it could have seen the terror-stricken face of the object under the mosquito net, it might have changed direction and purpose. I did not sleep well that night.

In the morning I found an opened tin of meat lying on the floor bearing indentations made by the visitor's teeth. If I had known then the size of those teeth, I would not have been so disparaging about the reluctance of the boys to answer my shouts. When I had asked them why they had not answered my shouts they said they had not heard me. But when I mentioned the visit of the lynx they said, "Oh yes - it was a big cat." At this I did not feel so bad about shouting as they had obviously been as perturbed as myself

At another small village school where I spent the night, I found it had one disturbing feature. As I was preparing for bed a colony of bats came out of their roosting places, no doubt attracted to the insects which, in turn, had been attracted to my lamp. What concerned me most of all was their propensity to void their bowels in flight. In the confines of the school it was not an acceptable feature, for my mosquito net was soon showing evidence of this by the droppings which patterned it. I imagined myself waking in the morning with a really nasty taste in my mouth, should I have slept with my mouth open. I organised the boys in a bat disposal exercise to prevent this from happening and which was quite successful. After extinguishing the lamp their reduced presence was acceptable.

The next morning we examined the women and girls. One young mother was standing in front of me and her baby's upper lip was covered with a thick mucous. With the action born of practice the mother placed her mouth over the mucous, sucked and then spat it out on the ground. I was surprised at this innovative solution, but not shocked. It was a matter of effective expediency, on a par with children of my youth who, not having a handkerchief, wiped their nose on their sleeve.

Another village appeared, at first acquaintance, to be a delightful spot but the prospective air of tranquillity was spoilt by the presence of a large number of flies. These, unfortunately, were a species of horse-fly, carried by herds of antelope or buffalo. They had the usual silent approach and soft landing, so that you were given no warning that they were around until you were bitten. I was sat outside one day enjoying a cup of tea, when I noticed a fly about to enter the leg of my shorts. My immediate reaction spilt my tea, as I shook the bottom of my shorts to deter the intruder from leaving a painful legacy of its visit. A general violent slap would possibly have resulted in more severe anatomical damage than the fly which, to my relief, flew away.

While we were there Dawedi decided to set up as a roadside trader. He had obviously planned for this, having collected over a period of time empty tins and bottles. These were displayed for the attention of passing villagers and were available in exchange for sweet potatoes. He had come away from Lui with a large bag of groundnuts, so when he came to me for an advance in his wages, I suggested he sell some of his nuts. He was shocked at this suggestion, pointing out the market price was no good at the moment. One of the SMS drivers, who had taken us about in the early days of the survey, had gone one better than Dawedi and traded salt with the bush natives, this commodity being in short supply out of town and somewhat of a luxury.

Christmas was upon us and I spent several days in Juba resthouse, where I met the only other occupant who suggested we go over to the Governor's house. It was the custom at this time of the year for free drinks to be dispensed. Back at the resthouse I had lunch and then relaxed with a book and a luxury I had allowed myself - a cigar - a box of which I had given to myself as a Christmas present. Then, for a while, I was at peace with the world.

Break over, we loaded up with petrol and supplies and set out on the long road to Terakeka. This lay on the banks of the Nile, about eighty miles north of Juba. The rains had finished late, preventing us from taking the shorter route, so we had to take the longer journey, for the most part over reasonable dirt roads, but covering 330 miles. I stopped at Mundri on the way and told them I would call on my return, then pulled in at a small village to stay the night. We examined a small number of people the next morning before going on to Terakeka. The road to Terakeka branched off right from what had been the original road and now became alternately rocky and sandy, with long grasses and stunted bush on either side. We found Terakeka to consist mainly of a police post, manned by a sergeant and two constables, who were responsible for fifty prisoners. About a hundred yards upstream was a Nile-steamer station with two large sheds and supplies of wood for the steamers. There were several such stations along the route of the steamers and men were employed in cutting wood into five-foot lengths and stacking it in neat piles at the water's edge. Slightly to the north of this were the scattered animals of a Mandari cattle camp.

The resthouse was one of the more substantially built, brick-walled structures with a central dining area, two small bedrooms (one at each end of the building) and a low-roofed veranda at the river end. An additional luxury were the mosquito-wired windows. Standing outside the entrance were two seers (porous stone jars) that were filled daily with water which slowly filtered through into containers. This was then boiled before being used for drinking. There was accommodation for the boys and a small kitchen. I slept indoors cognizant of the fact that crocodiles were not so very far away, although the steep banks at this point were a deterrent. I didn't know if crocodiles sleepwalked but if they did, I did not wish to be on their passage. I knew they were nearby for I came across one about three feet long, sleeping in the sun on the surface of the water. I disturbed its slumbers and it submerged.

The Mandari cattle camp was not far away. The dusty track of ground was studded at intervals by short wooden stakes, to which were tethered the cattle. A long pole was prominent in the centre and from the top flew a type of flag. During the day the cattle were taken to water and pasture, returning at early evening. Looking around the outskirts of the camp one morning I was flabbergasted to see several men standing behind the cows, staring at the animals' rears. The reason for this behaviour was soon made clear when, as a beast urinated, a man placed his head in the stream of urine and washed his hair. This gave the hair a reddish tinge and it was easy to pick out those who indulged in this practice. The men made it quite clear that they did not want me to photograph this ritual, so I photographed a boy milking instead. As he squirted the milk into a gourd some went over his body, washing away the dust (which was commonly smeared on) to disclose the black skin beneath. When we examined the workers at the steamer-station we were obliged to ask them to wash all over before they could be examined.

47. Boys washing in Nile

48. Nile Steamer & Barges – Terakeka

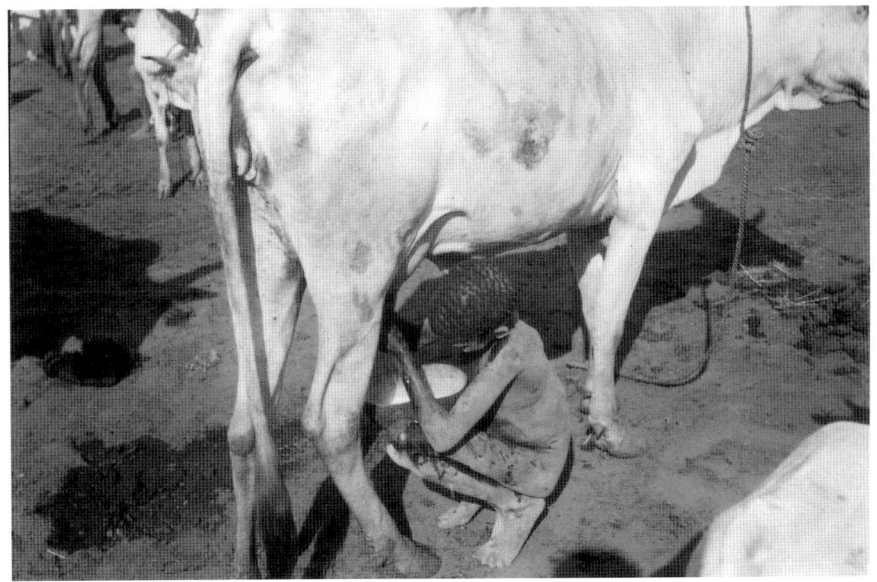

49. Boy milking – Terakeka

50. Man milking - Terakeka

51. Cattle camp – Terakeka

52. Mandari Hut

53. Dawedi – with Guinea Fowl – Terakeka

54. Farewell Dance

55. Farewell Dance

56. Rest house – Terakeka

57. Mandari Dry Season Camp – Boys wading out into river

During the initial stages of the Terakeka survey the chief was absent and his people uncooperative, so we awaited his return which was expected shortly. But when we saw him the position was not improved; if anything it worsened for the chief made it quite clear he had no intention of allowing the people of his village to be examined. So we were obliged to leave. However, we did manage to inspect a few stragglers, but to all intents and purposes our visit was a failure. I mentioned this to John Hannah when I returned to Juba and he said that his office experienced the same problem.

In spite of this disappointment at Terakeka, we had an uplift in spirits on the return to Tali. We were able to inspect some thirteen villages of various sizes - all Mandari. These were not readily reachable by road in the wet season and should they become accessible during the dry season, then many of the Mandari would have gone with their cattle to a source of water and pasture. However, in this case we were fortunate enough to have examined 1,196 persons in villages which did not appear on the maps with which I had been supplied. Fortunately, I was able to identify them from notes I had retained from my report.

Two things stood out in my memory about these villages. We were returning one day from one small village with the sub-chief, when we saw two girls approaching. They were wearing, rather unusually, long sari-type cloaks, draped around them. We stopped, at the sub-chief's instigation, then went with him to the girls when, I assumed, he explained we would like to examine them. He obviously knew the girls, who were about 17 years old, so we stood by while they laughed and joked together. Then, one of the girls slipped off her cloak, revealing a completely naked body. This was entirely unexpected and while the sub-chief gazed with obvious delight I, on the other hand, had a problem. The front of my shorts was protruding like a horizontally erected bell-tent. Turning away from the others I muttered to Andrea to carry on while I returned to the seclusion of the lorry. 'It's time you went on leave.' I thought, as I limped away, hoping I would not be needed to give an opinion. Anyhow, I seemed to have given an impromptu opinion already.

The second incident occurred at a village not far from Tali. I happened to mention that this was my last inspection before I went home. The next thing I knew was that drums began to beat and some of the people we had recently examined were dancing. I asked Andrea what it was all about and he said it was a Farewell Dance. I felt myself becoming emotional so I walked away a little and pretended to be adjusting my camera, then turned and recorded the spectacle on film as a pleasurable memory.

Tali, centre of the Mandari tribe's territory, was on the west bank of the Nile and some 200 miles west of Juba. The latter confirmed upon a multi-armed signpost, with other details. Such as:

Cape Town	4051 miles
London	5860 miles
Juba	225 miles
Terakeka	91 miles

The large brick-built resthouse was approached along a road lined with tall, thickly foliaged Kapok trees. It contained spacious rooms and mosquito-wired windows and doors. There was a brick kitchen and a separate building for the boys. There was a supply of water from a local well, delivered each morning by two or three prisoners from the police station.

The Mandari huts were built on a platform, four or five feet above the ground, supported at each corner with stout poles, and with a ladder-like entry walk to the hut's entrance. The open area beneath the hut was used as a kitchen, there being ample room for the women to light their fire and to grind corn, or cassava root between stones. The Mandari tradition of spreading their huts over a wide area made our work laborious. But this might be the least of our problems. Upon coming to the outskirts of one village we found no one to be seen except for an aged woman and a small child.

The old woman told us that the rest of the villagers had gone to a wedding feast - a day's walk away! Number of people examined that morning - two.

Native children had their various jobs to do within the community and you found the boys herding cattle, goats and sheep. Sometimes they could be seen sitting on high platforms among the crops, complete with their slings and a supply of stones, with which they kept at bay any animals such as boar and baboon, who might feed on the crop. Girls were more commonly seen looking after small children or fetching water in gourds balanced on their heads.

But the boys could be mischievous at times. Such as when we visited a small village and were driven off by a swarm of wild bees. They were wilder than usual because several boys had thrown sticks at their hive. This particular hive was situated in a tall tree on the edge of the open ground where we had not long before examined some people. The hive was elongated and cigar-shaped, about ten inches in diameter at its largest end, and constructed from tightly interwoven strips of bamboo and blocked at one end. The sides of the hive were sealed with mud to make them weatherproof. They were placed in the branches of trees at varying heights above the ground. When the bees first appeared I noticed several youths under the tree containing the hive, with sticks in their hands. It was obvious that they had disturbed the bees by throwing sticks at the hive. I puffed furiously at my pipe to deter our attackers, but to no avail, and we hurriedly climbed into the lorry and made off. I remembered that a surveyor had told me that he had been forced to leave his work because of their attack which had been known to kill people.

Our seven days at Tall passed quickly. Thoughts of leaving soon on the Nile steamer lingered in my mind. It was also time to remember the good times. The laughter of the people; the rugged grandeur of sand, bush and time sculptured hills; ways that were both quaint and exasperating; hands extended in greeting which cushioned moments when you felt alone.

I called in on the Mays at Mundri and unloaded my trek-box, which I had promised them. Then on to Lui where I made brief farewells to the Roscoes, before continuing on to Juba to finalise arrangements for my journey home. Also, to collect my trek allowance of 60 piastres a day for the last time. This to be used, as so often before, on a meal at the Juba Hotel.

Chapter 19

Upon my return to Juba I compiled my monthly survey report for the last time. I gave unwanted clothing to Dawedi and my general duties boy, together with a month's wages, as was the custom when you went on leave. I visited Andrea at Luri Rokwe to take him my deck-chair and where I met his wife and child. They appeared to be comfortable in their new house, with its large single room. No drastic change had taken place since my earlier visit concerning the state of the sanitation there. The problem had worsened since the Government had begun treating the patients with DDS. The leprosarium at Lui, giving proof that the treatment worked, encouraged many people to apply for treatment.

In between my absences from Juba on survey I had sometimes visited the Boltons, whom I had first met on the Nile steamer. On my last evening they kindly invited me to a meal prior to my boarding the steamer at the beginning of my homeward journey. It was dark when I made my way on board and, as I was sharing a cabin, I undressed in the dark as quickly as possible in case one of the bunks was occupied. In spite of the overhead fan the cabin was hot and stuffy. I was disturbed later by my cabin companion who, not particular about his entry, switched on the light and stomped about, before collapsing on his bunk. He also snored. Next morning we introduced ourselves to each other. His background was rather cosmopolitan, being of Syrian parentage but born in Greece, who was now representing a French interest in the Belgian Congo and travelling between Africa and Europe. I never found out what this rather worried-looking fat man was selling.

Among the other passengers I recognised several people from

Juba and a red-headed Dr Henry Farrel, going on leave from the Azande district. There was also a lanky, bespectacled individual, with a vague expression (mostly cultivated for the bewilderment of others) whom I had seen walking around Juba during the Christmas period. I had assumed him to be one of the American team working in the area. A mistake on my part, due to his wearing American style rimless glasses. In actual fact he was English and working for a Kenyan organisation specialising in boring for water. His contract was to put down bore-holes in the Khartoum area. The remainder of the passengers consisted of a party of Swiss tourists - all doctors of science - a German couple, a British M.P. and his wife, and finally, a Northern Sudanese school-teacher and his wife. We shared two decks of the steamer, which had a mosquito-wired lounge and a well-ventilated dining area. Those who did not have cabins on the steamer were provided with spacious cabins on one of the accompanying barges, secured to the steamer.

The forty or so native passengers ate, slept and did what best they could to make themselves comfortable for the seven day trip, on one of the partly enclosed barges pushed before the steamer and so placed to prevent the steamer itself from running aground. When we left Juba the mornings were noisy with the crowing of a dozen or so cockerels, caged at the rear of one barge. The volume of noise coming from them diminished more and more as we progressed northwards until, at Kosti where we disembarked, but a solitary bird remained to greet the day, the others having been eaten.

We passed downstream with the sparsely vegetated bank of the

Nile on the western side. On the first morning of our journey, we saw little wildlife apart from a few small buck and a group of baboon. Not forgetting the indigenous crocodile and hippo. Later the steamer station of Terakeka came into view and it was somewhat curious to see the place from a different angle and without the problems we had faced there. Several miles further on we passed close to one of the Mandari cattle camps on an island in the east channel of the river, equidistant to Terakeka and Gemmeixa. The river there was exceptionally shallow and several Mandari boys had waded out to near the centre of the waterway. We scraped the near bank with one of our protective barges causing it to tack rather alarmingly, almost sending one of the white-robed Northerners, sitting in front of the barge, overboard.

Further along, where the Nile resumed a single passage once more, the view of the banks was one of scattered trees and shrubs, now and again relieved by the presence of birds and crocodile. The latter, quite numerous in places, lay on sandbanks, or close in to the higher banks of the river. Dozing, with mouths wide open, they ignored the Zic-zac birds who seemed to tempt fate by entering the mouths to remove bits of food and other debris from the crocodiles' teeth. Sometimes the reptiles were disturbed by our passing as small tidal waves engulfed them. One small crocodile was washed along the line of the bank in a swirl of legs and foam. Flocks of riverside birds took off in a flurry of flight as they were disturbed. Sometimes, at sunset, the birds presented a swirling mass against the darkening sky as they made their way to their nesting places.

One of the Swiss noticed a small shelter standing among the papyrus growth on the bank. My Syrian-Greek cabin mate was standing close to him and evidently was asked what it was. The traveller licked his lips and went into an elaborate explanation of it being a totem of sorts. Hungry for facts, the Swiss swallowed the story. I was sat facing the pair, within hearing distance, and my face must have betrayed my feelings at this balderdash. The traveller looked at me, became confused, before looking hurriedly away, leaving the Swiss gazing with fascination at the structure until it was lost to view. Later the traveller came over to me and after making rather prosaic conversation for a few minute, finally said "You may have heard me talking to the Swiss."

I nodded.

"Of course," he continued, "I had to tell him something. They are like children these people, always asking questions. They expect an ordinary shelter to have strange and mystical connections, because it is in Africa."

The Swiss, no doubt, was glad to take this fiction home with him. But it was not long before he would have a different story to take home. The Swiss were here, there and everywhere with their cameras. It was about this time that I dropped my camera, causing me to lose four films of this part of the trip. The keenness of the Swiss to take photographs caused a disturbance before long. Several of the group were not very diplomatic in their approach to someone they wished to photograph. This method was not acceptable by a group of schoolboys who, both educated and fully clothed, did not wish to be seen adjacent to naked tribesmen. It was also likely that the Swiss had offered them money to pose for them. I had heard one of the Swiss asking one of the Northern Sudanese crew, who served behind the bar, if he could have "a pounds worth of ten piastre coins to give to the natives for photographs". The money must have been handed over with choice mutterings in Arabic.

The Swiss, at this stage, should have resorted to a telephoto lens. From the rail I looked back over the land to where a Northerner was approaching several natives, wearing nothing but their spears, even the business end of these was naked. Reaching them, I saw him indicating their naked personal parts and then pointing up at the sky, obviously telling his listeners that unless they covered themselves up the wrath of Allah would fall upon them. Which probably left the admonished, being Pagan, wondering what it was all about. It wasn't long before the Swiss cameras were out again before the steamer was leaving and this time the boys, who were on shore, threw stones at them, striking one of the women. While conceding that there had been a certain amount of provocation on the part of the Swiss, by failing to assess the situation, in no way could the throwing of stones be condoned. The engineer of the steamer, when the steamer stopped at Tonga, telephoned to the Governor at Malakal asking for an investigation into the incident. As a result of an investigation five of the schoolboys were convicted of assault and received ten lashes each. A further ten boys were given six strokes each.

My cabin companion was not at all happy with the situation for his large saloon car was on one of the accompanying barges and he was sure that it would be sabotaged. "They'll put sand in the engine or petrol tank." he worried. Then, unable to contain himself, he gave way to the strain he was generating and went off below to make sure that all was well. He had a boy who had travelled with him from the Congo, looking after the car, but felt convinced that he would be 'sabotaged' too. From then on he developed an 'anti-Swiss' complex, which he nurtured for the rest of the trip.

On quiet days I spent time on deck musing over memories of Dawedi, smiling to myself as I recalled some of Dawedi's exploits. One of my favourites concerned an old gramophone, when I was staying at the Roscoes' in their absence. The records available were old and an eclectic choice, had they belonged to one person, but it was quite reasonable to assume them to have been left behind by people who had once lived at Lui. One record I played was Solviegs's song from Peer Gynt. Not exactly music for a moment of the 'blues'. But that all changed when Dawedi, in the kitchen, turned the piece into a duet with the singer. He mimicked the woman's voice with little touches of his own, paraphrasing, or should I say 'paranoting', so that the combination made me forget a low mood. It was something I liked to put on the turntable when I needed my spirits raised. In a different vein a favourite of mine, Paul Robeson, was treated in very much the same way but aimed at the low notes, seldom heard in African singing. I wondered what Dawedi would have thought had I told him that the singer was a black man. I never told him and continued to enjoy his attempts to satirize.

Sometimes I talked to the driller. One thing I had noticed was that when he was speaking to someone and asked them a controversial question, or gave a contentious answer, he always put his tongue in his cheek. That he was doing so could quite clearly be seen. An exhibition which confirmed the 'tongue in cheek' to be a fact. But mostly he and I discussed photography and he once mentioned a printer's I myself used in Khartoum, who were not adverse to 'stealing' photographs for their own gain. It made me think of a film of mine containing a selection of various types of ant-hills which were reported as being spoilt by 'the light getting into the film'. The spoilt film was not returned so I could not confirm this for myself.

At evening there was nothing much to do or see so most passengers spent the evening in the dining saloon. Here we played cards, drank and talked. The M.P. and his wife usually played Bridge with the Jacks, after which they held the inevitable inquest. My evenings were less exacting - playing Rummy or Whist with the driller.

For two or three days we travelled through papyrus, growing outwards from the river on both sides as far as one could see. Often the only signs of life were black and white fish-eagles perched upon the posts at the water's edge. The posts were marked at intervals with lines which allowed a check upon the river levels. Egypt, relying so very much on the Nile's water further north, had an agreement with Great Britain which allowed the former's River-control teams to constantly check the river's levels. One of these teams was stationed at Juba.

Seven days after we had left Juba the steamer passed the swing bridge at Kosti. From here we took the train to Khartoum. Neither Henry Farrel nor myself had made arrangements for accommodation in Khartoum and after unsuccessfully trying several hotels we eventually obtained a double room at a Greek hotel. Or, at least, the proprietor said it was a room but we found it to be more like an upstairs dungeon. As it was situated in the centre of the building there were no windows in the room, which necessitated our having to leave the light on during the day. Not only that, we were next to the bathroom with its water-echoing plumbing.

In the evening we were all invited to the Jacks' house for drinks and then Henry and myself were invited out to dinner with the German couple at the Palace Hotel. The hotel lounges were frequented by the local European populace, supplemented by casual visitors and tourists. Beneath the sheltered frontage with its pillars, Sudanese merchants and dealers in ivory, ebony, silverwork, brassware, silks and carpets etc. displayed their wares on the stone floor. I showed an interest in some carved ivory animals. Immediately the dealer began his sales talk, asking far too much in my opinion.

"Why," I said. "Things are half the price in Omdurman."

"No – No," the other protested. "They are the same price. The same as Omdurman. I know."

"And I'll know tomorrow when I go there." I rejoined and passed on into the hotel.

After our meal at the hotel we went on to a cabaret, where the main attraction turned out to be a belly-dancer. Our German companion was paying for the drinks and our glasses always seemed to be filled. Not being used to drink, due on the whole to my rather penny-pinching way of life during the survey, I was forced to leave the table at one stage to be sick in the toilet. When I returned, the belly-dancer began her dance, or rather, display, for her clothing was minimal. We saw little of the climax of the dance because by this time those who wished to do so were standing on their tables. In our condition it would have been foolish to attempt this, so we had to imagine the rather erotic squirming taking place on the floor, encouraged by the onlookers. This also was the end of our evening and, leaving our hosts, we staggered off to find a taxi back to our hotel. Henry was sick in the taxi and we left the driver, holding several compensatory pounds in his hand, bemoaning the state of his vehicle and the potential loss of fares that evening.

Next morning I was awakened early by a rather despairing voice saying, "Oh, my God!" Followed by a more desperate diagnosis of, "Oh, my God! I'm dying." The doctor's head rolled from side to side, seeking comfort. I wasn't feeling too good myself. There was a heavy stale odour of vomit, most of it rising from Henry's suit which had been thrown loosely over a chair the night before. When the 'boy' answered our bell with the morning tea, Henry asked him to take away the suit to be cleaned. The 'boy' picked it up and, if he had belonged to another faith, would quite possibly have crossed himself, but he compromised by holding it at some length with obvious distaste.

When we visited Omdurman we had first to cross the bridge over the White Nile and from there watched the White and Blue Niles converge and run side by side in the same channel as they passed northwards from Omdurman. At Omdurman market the first shop I entered contained the merchant I had previously seen at the Palace Hotel. He greeted me triumphantly.

"Everything the same price." He said with a self-satisfied smile. I was forced to concede that this was so.

The shop was built from street level, two steps above the dusty roadway along which came a continuous crowd of assorted tourists and white-robed locals. Shop owners stood outside sheltered doorways shouting their wares as they tried to attract potential trade. The shouting I could have done without for I was still felling the effects of the night before. Dark glasses hadn't helped so to ease my discomfort, I spent most of the time inside the shops to avoid the heat and glare of the sun. Two things stood out from that visit, the handbag sellers and the ivory carvers. The handbag tout pounced upon our party waving the most revolting bag I have ever seen, then or since. The bag was made from crocodile skin but the finished article showed a lack of taste to western eyes, for a small crocodile's head was utilised as the flap. Its teeth still remained, set in a fixed grin or grimace. It was a pleasant change to look in at the ivory carvers. This consisted of a rather crude shack, on the floor of which sat six or seven craftsmen shaping animals from the basic lump of tusk. Without a model to copy they shaped the piece by first a rough file, sending ivory filings everywhere. It was amazing to see how quickly the shape of an elephant appeared from the original nondescript lump. This was near-finished with a fine file and then finally polished. I bought several pieces.

Later that day Henry and I moved out of the room in what must have been the annex, into the main part of the hotel. Having been shown my new room, which I had to share, I was somewhat relieved to find my room-mate to be the driller. We went our individual ways for a few days and I was constantly amazed at the driller bringing back a pack of dates on most days. He never seemed to eat them and after a while the air was filled with a heavy, sweet aroma of dates every time he opened his wardrobe, where he had hoarded them.

Later he told me about himself. Of his coming out to Kenya from England, to work for practically nothing on a farm, eventually leaving to join a drilling company. He showed me a photograph of a rather striking looking Syrian girl he had known in England, when she had nursed him in hospital when he had a broken leg.

"I would have married her," he said, "when I'd saved enough money out here. Then her sister wrote to say that she was to marry an American. So I'm in no hurry to go home now."

He glanced up and looked out of the window. Coming to life to say "So that's where she lives." Half to himself.

"Who?" I prompted. "Where who lives?"

"A girl." he answered. "A Syrian girl who works in a shop in town."

"I would have thought you had enough of Syrian girls." I said. The realisation came. "So that's the shop where you've been buying all those dates?"

"Yes." He grinned. "I couldn't very well go into the shop and buy nothing. I don't like dates myself, as you may have gathered. So I'll send them home to my father. He likes dates."

"If I were you, I'd keep well clear of it." I cautioned.

"Well" rejoined the driller optimistically. "They can't all be the same - and I'll be working in this area for several months."

Early next morning he went out with the intention of seeing the girl and asking her for a date (on the social side for a change). When he came back I saw the disappointment in his face, for the girl's father had been in the shop and the only date he had got was in a box. "If you don't hurry that wardrobe will be bursting with dates."

But he refused to admit defeat and said he would go down to the shop again later. He returned looking somewhat dejected. I waited for him to speak.

"No luck," he admitted at last "When I asked her if she would come out with me, she laughed. Then asked me if I were an American."

"Must have been your rimless glasses."

"Probably" agreed the driller. "Anyway" he continued "When I told her I wasn't an American but English - do you know what she said?"

"What did she say?"

"She said that she would have gone out with me had I been an American but as I was English - No!"

"It seems to me," I reflected, "that Syrian girls have an interest in the American way of life."

"Looks that way," agreed the driller "but there are bound to be other girls around somewhere."

"Maybe it would be better to get a dog." I proposed.

"It might be," he conceded, "but you can't kiss a dog."

There was no answer to that.

I wasn't to know whether the driller's quest was successful or not as shortly the train left for Port Sudan. Two days travel over desert, with nothing to see but a few huts or tents, insignificant features of the vast landscape. Each morning the train was stopped to allow the Muslim crew to dismount and prostrate themselves at the side of the track, to say their prayers. This was followed by a general sweeping through the corridors of the carriages, to remove the large quantities of sand which had infiltrated throughout the night.

At Port Sudan the customs officers conducted a slow examination of our luggage. When my turn came, I disclosed I had nothing to declare apart from a few ivory animals, purchased at Omdurman. Henry, a little to my right, was having the beginning of an argument with another officer, presumably over the time he was taking. As I turned to walk to the ship which was at the dockside not far away, I overheard a fragment of conversation concerning some small drums Henry possessed.

"Would you open up those drums, Sir, so that I can see inside?"

I passed quickly on. It obviously did not pay to argue.

In a way I had not told the whole truth, when asked if I had anything to declare. I did - but it was an abstract thing consisting of my memories. The final compilation of which has taken me over fifty years and with them is the hope that I gave Africa as much as she gave me.

Epilogue

Upon my return to England I spent several days at home before going to BELRA's London office, where I began work on the Sudanese Survey report. Fortunately, for me, Dr Cochrane was there and I was grateful for his help and advice, as to putting the results into an acceptable format. I shared his office for a few days and one day he surprised me by asking where I would be going to work next. I was obliged to tell him that when my assignment was completed I would be resigning. He did not pursue the matter, somewhat to my relief, although the reason was simple enough, to me anyhow. I had, on the whole, and in spite of the early setbacks with transport, enjoyed the challenge of survey work. In contrast, I had found the comparative static involvement of leprosarium work at Lui confining, with a sense of loss of freedom. Realising that the degree of commitment required for this aspect of the work was something I could not wholeheartedly comply with, I would not have had the dedication. Sometimes, when the feeling of being hemmed in became too much, I walked to the top of a nearby hill, overlooking Lui, and from where I would gaze over the trees into the distance. If I were lucky, the scene would be enhanced by a cooling breeze.

58. Scene overlooking Lui

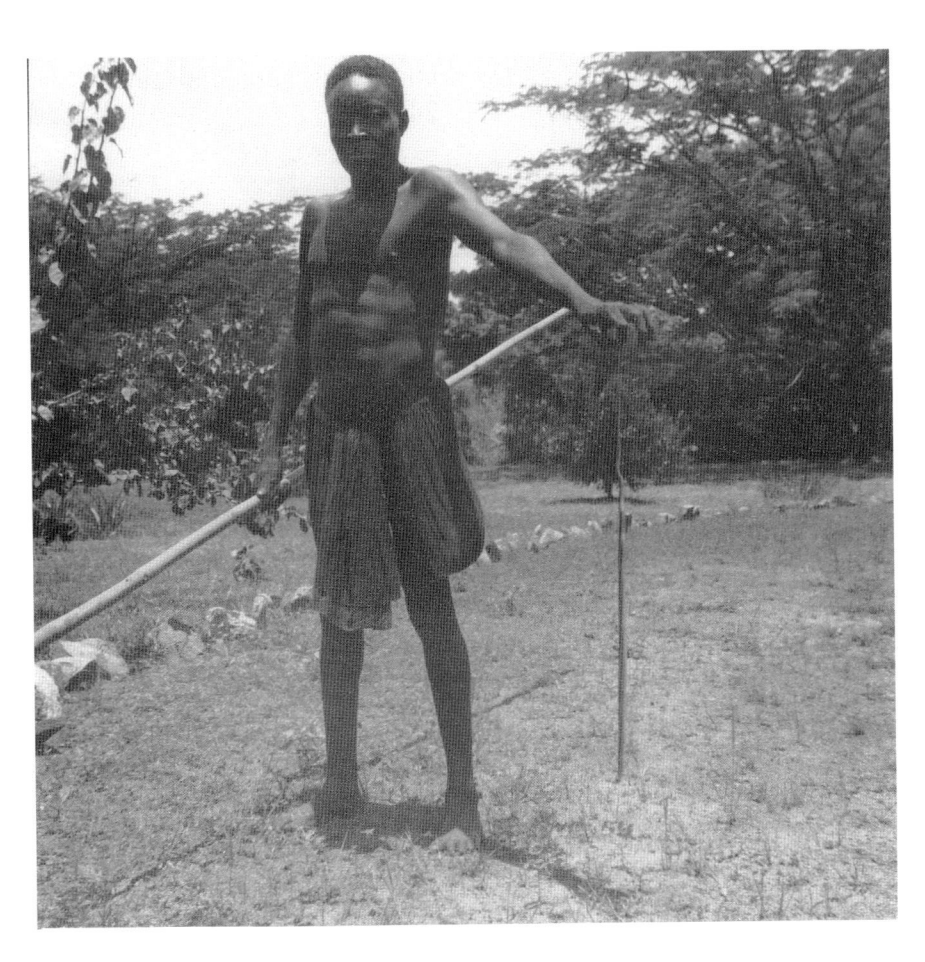

59. Gardener with snake - Lui

On completion of the report the final figures were identified
Number of persons examined -   24,098.0
Number of cases of leprosy -   1,102.0
Incidence per thousand -   45.7
Number of male cases -   537.0
Number of female cases -   515.0

Number in each age group

0 - 6	59
7 - 16	300
17 - 26	105
27 - 36	300
37 - 46	222
47 - 56	87
57 - 66	29

Types of leprosy cases noted

Lepromatous	155	14.0% of cases
Tuberculoid	820	74.4% of cases
Indeterminate	127	11.5% of cases

Comparison of tribal incidence per thousand

Tribe	Examined	Number of cases	Incidence per thousand
Lokoya	5,919	317	53
Bilinga	1,753	107	61
Bari	9,086	460	50
Mandari	3,221	77	23.9*
Fejula	1,500	54	36
Nyambura	390	16	41**
Juba (mixed)	1,961	63	32

---

* This low figure to be expected due to the Mandari life-style.
** A high incidence due mainly to the fact that only three villages were available for inspection in Equatorial Province.

The report shows the areas of high incidence, suggesting where treatment centres might be usefully located. Individual villages were recorded, together with basic background details, creating a sufficient foundation upon which to build.

Troubles in the Southern Sudan now (2008) and especially in earlier years, have made the results obsolete. Since the late 1950s more than 2,000,000 Southerners have died as a result of bombing and other acts of war, famine and disease. A tendency to ethnic cleansing, as shown by the Government's turning a blind eye to what is happening in Darfur, where the state-backed militia - the Janaweed - terrorises the population, to the extent of raping women when they go to obtain water for their families. There is also a hidden trade in slavery, exposed by a Nuban girl, Mende Nazer, in her BBC audio book, 'Slave', which shows all to clearly the reactions of a 12 year old girl who, together with others, and in spite of their being Muslims, were abducted by Northern Muslims. They were raped by their captors prior to being taken to the North and sold to traders.

An older girl, Halina Bashir, describes her experiences in her book 'Tear in the Desert', a vastly different experience from that of Mende Nazer. Since a child Halina had expressed the wish to become a doctor. Her father, a successful business man, was able to see that his daughter received the necessary education to obtain a place at Khartoum University to study medicine.

Here she recognised that she and other Southerners were despised by many at the university and herself more so when she voiced her opinions concerning the Government treatment of the South and the conflicts there.

Because of this she was only granted a minimum pass for her final exam. When she queried this, she was told by a Government official that it was because of her poor attendance at lectures. It was such a blatant lie and when her tutor, who a little time earlier had told her she would gain a good degree, backed this decision, she was furious.

Back in Darfur she was not offered an appointment for some time until, at long last, she was offered a position away from her own district. It was here that she was eventually arrested for treating fighters on both sides of the conflict taking place. Her interrogators demanded the name of all Southerners she had treated. This she refused to do.

Several days later her hatred of the North intensified when a group of Janaweed attacked a local girls' school and raped over 40 young girls, 7-14 years of age. As there was no other doctor available Halina was faced with having to treat the horrendous internal injuries alone. Injuries made all the worse by the fact that the girls had been circumcised, as was the custom.

A week later she was seized by Secret Police who, over a period of several days, beat and raped her several times before she was finally released. The one in charge of the group whispered to her

"Now you know how the others felt." And this was so, for she herself had suffered the operation as a child.

Returning home her brothers, seeing her condition and the experience she had suffered, decided that they would join the rebels. Their father said he would negotiate for them but, before this could take place, their village was attacked by five helicopter gunships and laid to waste by this and a screaming horde of Janaweed on horseback. Their father saw them safely away and returned alone to the village. They later found his body among the ruins.

Her two brothers joined the rebels shortly afterwards. It was suspected that the Government were looking for Halina so her mother persuaded her to leave the country. She gave her daughter what money she had for travel to England.

The Guardian reported in July 2008 that Abu Dhabi is to develop 30,000 hectares of land for potential farmland in the Sudan, this, as a first step in ensuring food security for the emirate. The area concerned would be watered from the Nile.

It is a scheme which has come under criticism by the UN's Food and Agricultural Organisation (FAO) for wealthy countries and companies trying, and often succeeding, in securing food supplies from the developing world. This is particularly so in the case of the Gulf States where negotiations have taken place to lease large areas of farmland in the Sudan and Senegal, while Kenya is being approached by Qatar who is rich in oil and gas but deficient in arable farmland. It is reported that deals have been struck in 2008 to grow rice in Cambodia, wheat in the Sudan and vegetables in Vietnam.

The Sudanese Government has welcomed this arrangement offering use of the land, hoping to benefit from future business links. The area primarily concerned is that where years of war have prevented local development. Now 80% of this potential farmland will be open to speculation, to the detriment of Southern tribes, and in particular the cattle tribes. These would lose most by these plans, because of their need to move cattle to water in the dry season. This new policy is certain to be met with resistance.

A similar case in point is Qatar's offer to fund a new £2.4bn port on an island belonging to Kenya; this, in return for a lease on 40,000 hectares of land on which to grow crops. Other Gulf States are also seeking large tracts of farmland. The Sudan and Senegal have already accepted proposals. Kenya itself already suffers from insufficient food supplies, in spite of the fact that the Government owns nearly 500,000 hectares of uncultivated land. An agreement to allow a local company to grow sugar cane would destroy what is considered to be communal land and would destroy its traditional use - that of the area's use for up to 60,000 cattle to graze in this delta area each dry season - a problem already encountered by the Sudan.

The FAO say that a previous project in the Sudan showed but limited benefits for local people.

A percentage of the profits from the sale of this book will be divided equally between Médecins Sans Frontiers and L.E.P.R.A.

The last in tribute to Jimmy Roscoe who, after arranging his family's return to England, returned to Lui. Here, in the 1950's, he endured the disturbances of Local conflict, including the bombing of Lui by northern aircraft. During which the colony church was destroyed.